SERGEY AVETISYAN

The Time of City Economics
Think about economics otherwise

First published by Independently published 2021

Copyright © 2021 by Sergey Avetisyan

All rights reserved. No part of this publication may be reproduced, stored or transmitted in any form or by any means, electronic, mechanical, photocopying, recording, scanning, or otherwise without written permission from the publisher. It is illegal to copy this book, post it to a website, or distribute it by any other means without permission.

Sergey Avetisyan asserts the moral right to be identified as the author of this work.

Sergey Avetisyan has no responsibility for the persistence or accuracy of URLs for external or third-party Internet Websites referred to in this publication and does not guarantee that any content on such Websites is, or will remain, accurate or appropriate.

Designations used by companies to distinguish their products are often claimed as trademarks. All brand names and product names used in this book and on its cover are trade names, service marks, trademarks and registered trademarks of their respective owners. The publishers and the book are not associated with any product or vendor mentioned in this book. None of the companies referenced within the book have endorsed the book.

Third edition

This book was professionally typeset on Reedsy.
Find out more at reedsy.com

To my mentors, colleagues, and students.

Contents

Preface ii
1 Introduction 1
2 City economics 3
3 Ordinary cities 6
4 Cultural city 10
5 Walkable city 16
6 Industrial city 21
7 Creative city 23
8 Consumer city 28
9 Green city 30
10 Healthy City 32
11 Megacity 36
12 Charter city 41
13 Startup city 43
14 Smart city 49
15 Happy city 56
16 Integral city 61
17 Future cities 64
18 Still same city 67
Notes 69
About the Author 81

Preface

There is no new words or concepts in this book, but it is a unique collection of ideas. What are we talking about when we talk about urban development? Do we need to know the particulars, the details?

This is a book about the urban economy. When I began writing it, I had in mind an "ideas book" of basic types to adapt as starting points to help us think about the urban economy.

Those types are presented in Chapters, 2 through 17.

However, you can't work through many of those models before a central question emerges "Why an urban economy?" Close behind is a related second question: "Why do governments encourage an urban economy (or not)?"

At the beginning to outline the theme of a book, I scribbled a list of the characteristics of a city whose economy I was thinking about. At the time, I wanted to clarify the city's nature for which this book's ideas are aimed.

However, as the two central questions above took shape, it became evident how thinking about governance was a central understanding of how the urban economy operates. To be clear, this book is not about how political outcomes shape markets' operation that in turn, organize activities within and between cities.

Considering the development of the city is not a straightforward task. It is so easy to overlook the evidence in front of us. For centuries we have been taught that the city was terrible for us, that it was the drain of our interagency, that it destroyed the old ways and traditions, split families and offered little in exchange but disorder, dirt and noise. This negative reading of the city has affected policy, literature, and architecture, sometimes disastrous. We are now an urban species. In the developed world, we have become used to this reality, but elsewhere, in Africa, Asia, Latin America, these urban quakes are being felt for the first time. We are in the midst of the last great human migration in history.

Today, we face a new set of challenges even more complex and pressing than ever before: climate change, unprecedented migration, the depletion of limited resources and a widely perceived decline in the civic values that hold our societies together. The consequences of a failure to acknowledge these problems are profound. Humanity stands at a tipping point between disaster and survival, and the city is the fulcrum upon which our future balances. This book is a rallying call for the city's reclamation from the sceptical grumbles and the stuck-in-the-mud municipal administrators. I believe that cities are good for us, and maybe the best means to ensure our survival.

As I will show in the following paragraphs, we have often misread the city development, which has informed how we have designed, planned and policed it. Often the aspects of the urban personality that have most disconcerted us are actually the most vitality signals. As a result, our home's best parts have been stifled and replaced by an idea of the city that has discouraged community, complexity, and creativity.

The book's main idea is that when policymakers concerning some concept of development, they must have in mind which kind of city they want to be created. One concept may not be suitable for all!

*Cities have the capability of providing something for everybody, only because,
and only when they are created by everybody.*

— JANE JACOBS —

1

Introduction

In most languages, at least in English, French and Spanish, the word "*city*" has both meanings. It can refer to both a political-administrative unit, as in the City of Paris and its generic usage, to an urban area. Borrowed from French *municipal*, from Latin *mūnicipālis* ("of or belonging to a citizen or a free town"), from *mūniceps* ("a citizen, an inhabitant of a free town"), from *mūnus* ("duty") + *capiō* ("to take").[1] In the German adage quoted earlier, referring to the historically liberating effects of cities, the word "*city*" is implicitly used to designate both a generic entity (an urban place) and an administrative-political unit. This use is valid in its historical context. In the Middle Ages and the Renaissance, "*cities*" in Germany, Italy and other parts of Western Europe often had separate charters, creating distinct institutional environments, which facilitated trade and economic activity.[2]

Cities were organized as independent corporations with, in essence, their own constitutions. By contrast, at that time, Russia had no Western-model corporate towns, no municipal law, and no maxims such as "*City air makes you free.*"[3] This may explain, in part, why Russia was later less successful in promoting economic growth.

The point is this: it is only valid to use the two meanings interchangeably where the term *"cities"* (i.e., urban areas) refers to distinct institutional environments that, in turn, significantly impact economic behaviour.[4] This is not the case in most nations today. While there are exceptions, such as the city-state of Singapore and several of the emerging mega-urban areas of East Asia (Jakarta, Hong-Kong and Pearl River in China), the role of *"cities"* (political-administrative definition) in most nations is mainly to deliver local public services. While local legislation and administrative regulations are key factors in determining a given region's investment climate and competitiveness, most of the legal-institutional environment remains national legislation or state/provincial legislation in federations.

2

City economics

City economics is a sub-field of economics that refers to the economic analysis of cities and touches on a broad range of topics, such as housing, transportation, land use, the cost and benefit of cities and urbanization, or the provision of local public goods like education.

City economics is the discipline that lies at the intersection of geography and economics. Urban economics explores utility-maximising households' location decisions and profit-maximising firms, and it shows how these decisions cause the formation of cities of different size and shape. The intersection of geography and economics defines the discipline of urban economics.[5] Economics explores the choices people make when resources are limited. Households make choices to maximise their utility, while firms maximise their profit. Geographers study how things are arranged across space, answering the question, *Where does human activity occur?*

Urban economics puts economics and geography together, exploring utility-maximising households' geographical or location choices and profit-maximising firms. Urban economics also identifies inefficiencies in location choices and examines alternative public policies to promote efficient decisions.⁶

The urban transformation has become a significant contributor to economic, demographic, social and environmental change.⁷ Twentieth-century urbanisation models were typically applied without full consideration of future outcomes and path dependencies, as the use of the private motor car and urban sprawl became dominant trends.⁸ In the twenty-first century, global urbanisation must be shaped and managed so that cities fully achieve their potential to increase prosperity and social cohesion, bring about improved environmental efficiency standards, citizen health and well-being, and strengthen international relations. If it is not managed, and if suitable local financing and investment tools are not achieved, rapid urbanisation could prove a significant threat to both modern society and the world's environmental fabric. The future form, functionality, appearance, and ambience of cities will directly impact most people's lives, whether they live in a town or not.⁹ The future city will not only impact on society but will also influence more comprehensive global environments and economies. In economics, the largest city markets have already grown more prominent than those of many nations. New York has an economy that is approximately the same size as Australia's and is the 12th largest globally. Even more modest cities eclipse some national economies – for example, Anchorage has a broader economy than Latvia.¹⁰ In the future, cities will be binding their roles as critical drivers of national, and sometimes even regional economies.

As we look forward, the fusion of economics and geography within the realm of urban economics becomes increasingly imperative. The dynamics of urban transformation have transcended mere spatial rearrangements; they now wield profound influence over economic, demographic, social, and environmental landscapes.

Reflecting on the twentieth century, we recognize that urbanization models were often employed without fully grasping their long-term consequences and path dependencies. The unchecked proliferation of private motor vehicles and the sprawl of urban areas epitomized this oversight. However, the twenty-first century demands a paradigm shift. Global urbanization must be guided by meticulous planning and management to harness cities' potential as engines of prosperity, social cohesion, and environmental sustainability.

Indeed, the future of cities is not merely a local concern but a global imperative. The choices made in urban planning and governance will reverberate far beyond city limits, impacting international relations, environmental integrity, and economic vitality. As exemplified by the economic prowess of cities like New York and Anchorage, urban centers are emerging as powerhouses rivaling national economies.

Looking ahead, cities are poised to become even more central to the fabric of global commerce and culture. They will not only shape the daily lives of their residents but also influence broader international dynamics. Thus, effective urban policy and investment strategies are crucial not only for the well-being of individual cities but also for the resilience and prosperity of nations and regions worldwide.

In summary, the convergence of economics and geography within urban economics provides a framework to navigate the complexities of urbanization in the twenty-first century. By embracing this interdisciplinary approach and implementing forward-thinking policies, we can ensure that cities fulfill their potential as catalysts for inclusive growth, environmental stewardship, and global prosperity.

3

Ordinary cities

Robinson suggests that instead of focusing solely on global cities or cities in developing nations, academic analysis and policy recommendations should prioritize what she refers to as "ordinary" cities. These cities, with their intricate, varied, and unique characteristics, offer valuable insights that can be applied across different contexts.

The ordinary city is a term coined, in human geography, by Ash Amin and Stephen Graham in an original article published in 1997.[11] Ordinary Cities forms the basis for a new, postcolonial framework for thinking about cities, one that cuts across the long-standing divide in urban scholarship between accounts of 'Western' and other kinds of cities, especially cities that have been labelled as 'Third World'. It is in the spirit of a postcolonial critique that Amin and Graham's book promotes the case for 'ordinary cities,' for an urban theory that draws inspiration from the complexity and diversity of city life, and urban experiences and urban scholarship across a wide range of different kinds of cities.[12] This is in strong contrast to much urban theory, which has taken its primary inspiration from cities in the West and has tended to privilege these places' individual experiences.[13]

Jennifer Robinson's *"Ordinary Cities"* delivers a powerful critique of the spatial division of academic theorization.[14] Her central thesis is that urban theory development has been hampered for too long by the assumed dichotomy between innovative *"global cities"* in rich countries and imitative "third world" cities in developing countries.[15] Robinson contends that theoretical insights cannot be based on a few wealthy cities' experiences only. A post-colonial field of urban studies should assume the potential for learning in a broad range of different settings.[16] For this reason, she envisages an urban theory that does not rest on pre-given categories of cities but on a cosmopolitan comparative that places all cities within the same analytical field. Within this field, the differences across and within cities must be considered diversity rather than exemplars of a hierarchical division. Robinson argues that it is not global cities or third-world cities central to academic analysis and policy recommendations. In all their complexity, diversity, and peculiarity, she calls *"ordinary"* cities to learn from different contexts.[17]

In the remainder of her book, Robinson examines the implications of her critical rethinking of the idea of modernity for academic theorization and policy development. First, Robinson criticises the world cities literature to emphasise a relatively small sector of the global economy and drop most cities in the world from its vision. Because of the focus on advanced business and producer services, cities like Lusaka or Kuala Lumpur largely fall off the world cities map, even though they are tied to the rest of the world through a wide range of economic activities such as the trade-in second-hand clothing or Islamic forms of global activity. As the world cities, literature reproduces hierarchical relations amongst cities where some urban places are defined as modern, and others need development. It is a problematic framework for theorization on cities, however, and policy development. Robinson elaborates this argument in the fifth chapter by analysing the Johannesburg 2030 vision for the city. To secure economic growth and improved service delivery in

Johannesburg, Robinson claims that a "city development strategy" has to start from a city-wide view of urban features that takes the diversity of needs and activities in poor and wealthy parts of the city seriously.[18] For this reason, Robinson calls, in the *Ordinary Cities'* last chapter, for theoretical repertoires that are appreciative of the diversity of cities. These have to focus on the close intertwining of social welfare and economic activities in both poor and rich cities by acknowledging that all cities are assembling and inventing diverse ways of being modern.

The concept of the "ordinary city," introduced by Ash Amin and Stephen Graham in 1997, marked a significant shift in urban scholarship, transcending traditional distinctions between "Western" and "Third World" cities. This postcolonial perspective underscores the diverse and complex nature of urban experiences, challenging the dominance of theories derived solely from affluent Western cities. Jennifer Robinson builds on this notion, advocating for an urban theory that embraces a cosmopolitan comparative approach, treating all cities as equal participants in urban studies.

Robinson's critique highlights the limitations of existing urban theory, particularly in the realm of world cities literature, which often prioritizes a narrow segment of the global economy while overlooking the diverse economic activities found in cities worldwide. By focusing solely on advanced business and producer services, many cities, such as Lusaka or Kuala Lumpur, are marginalized, perpetuating hierarchical divisions that hinder both theoretical understanding and policy development.

Using examples like the Johannesburg 2030 vision, Robinson emphasizes the importance of a more inclusive approach to urban development that acknowledges the varied needs and activities present in both affluent and impoverished areas of a city. Her call for theoretical frameworks that appreciate the diversity of urban experiences underscores the interconnectedness of social welfare and economic activities across all cities, regardless of their wealth or status.

In essence, Robinson's advocacy for ordinary cities challenges us to rethink our conceptual frameworks and recognize the richness and complexity inherent in urban life worldwide. By embracing diversity and adopting a more inclusive approach to urban theory and policy, we can pave the way for a more equitable and sustainable urban future.

4

Cultural city

City culture is aspects of life in a city that people enjoy and regards as valuable. Culture emerges over a city's history due to its residents' shared experiences, and a city may have more than one culture.

The discussion of urban issues often involves economic and political concerns. However, some of the more critical aspects of the new urban sociology emphasize greater attention to political economy. But this is not all there is to the new approach. People live in a symbolic world that is meaningful to them. They possess sentiments and ideas and attempt to communicate with others using common concepts.[19]

Social interaction in human societies is organized through the direct use of spoken or written language. A significant part, however, employs expressive symbols that are used to convey meanings.[20] One of the principal sources of extended life involves aspects of the built environment. Cities and suburbs are the sites of many subcultures—ethnic: religious, racial, gender-specific, and age-related. Neighbourhoods within the metropolis can readily be identified by objects that are signs of subcultural status. For example, ethnic areas of the city advertise themselves by the characters in front of restaurants, bakeries, speciality shops, and religious institutions. Architecture is often used to convey power and wealth, and in the States, government buildings using classical architecture are intended to display democratic ideals.[21]

People use such signs to orient themselves as they engage in urban life. The study of culture and objects' role as characters constitute a significant part of the new urban sociology. Sociologists have studied metropolitan life as culturally meaningful for some time. What is unique and different is the way such meanings are associated with objects in addition to words. For example, cities often try to develop an image that boosts attention to attract investment and tourists.[22]

Various images have been used, such as signs of industry ("Motor City"), symptoms of regional Urban Semiotics and the Built Environment. Many government buildings in the States use architectural elements from classical Greek architecture and are meant to recall ideas of Athenian democracy.[23] Learning how to read the urban environment is an example of urban semiotics. The U.S. Supreme Court building, situated on a hill with an entry reminiscent of the Slogans such as these are often linked to images or objects, such as a skyline or a graphic logo of some kind. In this way, a particular symbolic identity is created for a place that gives the impression that it is unique. The study of culture that links symbols to objects is called semiotics, and the particular subfield that studies the built environment in this manner is called spatial semiotics.[24] In the past, approaches to urban sociology have neglected the symbolic aspect of space, although some interesting early exceptions exist. The perspective we will follow integrates the symbolic nature of environments with more traditional factors that make up social behaviour, such as class, race, gender, age, and social status. Space, then, is another compositional factor in human behaviour. Scientists call this new perspective on urban life the sociospatial approach.[25]

Typical urban sociology books present several alternative ways of understanding sociospatial phenomena, or they present none at all and describe a succession of topics. However, the Lefebvrian turn in urban studies—including geography, urban planning, political economy, and sociology—developed as the *"socio-spatial approach"* to urban sociology. In the past, urbanists have regarded space as only a container of social activities. But this view is limited. The area contains actions and constitutes a part of social relations and is intimately involved in our daily lives.²⁶ It affects the way we feel about what we do. In turn, people alter space and construct new environments to fit their needs better. Hence, a dual relationship exists between people and space. On the one hand, human beings act according to social factors such as gender, class, race, age, and status within and in reaction to a given space. When a city converts a vacant lot into a basketball court, the type of activity and interaction of groups of persons within that space will change.²⁷

On the other hand, people create and alter spaces to express their own needs and desires. The sociospatial perspective is developed around the study of everyday life in contemporary urban society. It recognizes that the urban and suburban settlement spaces that make up the built environment are situated within a broader metropolitan region. We adopt a regional perspective to study the older central cities, suburban communities, and new growth poles that make up the twenty-first century's metropolitan region. Scientists call this new form of social space in the multicentered metropolitan area. We ask how and why multicentered urban areas in the states and across the globe came to be structured the way they are.²⁸

The sociospatial perspective emphasizes the interaction between society and space. Within the multicentered metropolitan region, groups differ from one another concerning lifestyle, attitudes, beliefs, and access to political power and influence. They have more or less influence on how social space is allocated and structured within and across the metropolitan region. To class, gender, race, and other social characteristics that define difference among groups in contemporary society, we add the element of space itself.[29] The spatial arrangements found in urban and suburban settlement space have both manifest and latent consequences: They influence human behaviour and interaction in predictable ways but also in ways The Sociospatial Perspective focuses our attention on how everyday life in the multinucleated metropolitan region is affected by the political economy of urban life— the interplay of cultural, political, economic, and social forces both within and outside of urban communities: The urban and suburban settlement spaces that comprise the built environment are part of a broader metropolitan region. It is necessary to adopt a regional perspective to understand the multinucleated metropolitan areas of the twenty-first century.[30]

The multinucleated metropolitan region is linked to the global capitalist system where decisions influence local areas' well-being made from the metropolitan, the national, or even the international level.[31]

Metropolitan development is affected by government policy and by developers, financiers, and other institutions in the real estate industry that creates incentives and opportunities that mould the behaviours, preferences, and choices of individual consumers. Everyday life is organized according to cultural symbols and material objects that are part of the built environment; these symbols and items are likely to have different meanings to different individuals or groups. Urbanists call the study of these symbols and objects urban semiotics.[32] The spatial arrangements found in urban and suburban settlement space have both manifest and latent consequences. They influence human behaviour and interaction in predictable ways; the original planner or developer may not have anticipated. Through their actions and interactions with others, individuals always alter existing spatial arrangements and construct new spaces to express their needs and desires.[33]

The original planner or developer may not have anticipated. Through their behaviours and interactions with others, individuals and groups always alter existing spatial arrangements and construct new spaces to express their needs and desires. The sociospatial perspective connects the dual relationship between people and plays with social factors based on individual behaviour.[34] However, this approach's most fundamental concept is settlement space, which refers to the built environment in which people live. Settlement space is both constructed and organized. It is made by people who have followed some meaningful plan to contain economic, political, and cultural activities. Within it, people manage their daily actions according to the expressive aspects of the constructed space. In subsequent chapters, we will discuss how socio-spatial factors determine the construction and use of settlement space. Over time we will also see how change has occurred and how socio-spatial factors, in turn, mould the built city development.

In the bustling urban landscape, where economic and political forces collide, lies a deeper layer of meaning awaiting discovery. In this riveting exploration of the city's heartbeat, we journey beyond the surface, delving into the rich tapestry of symbols and expressions that shape its identity.

From the towering skyscrapers to the quaint neighborhood streets, every corner of the city tells a story—a story of culture, heritage, and social dynamics. In this captivating narrative, we uncover the hidden language of urban life, where spoken words meet expressive symbols in a dance of communication.

Through the lens of urban semiotics, we decode the messages embedded in the city's architecture, signage, and street scenes. From the grandeur of government buildings to the humble storefronts of ethnic enclaves, each element speaks volumes about power, status, and identity.

But the story doesn't end there. As we navigate the urban landscape, we come to understand the intricate interplay between society and space. From the bustling city center to the sprawling suburbs, every inch of terrain is a battleground of social forces, shaping and reshaping the environment in a perpetual dance of influence.

In this groundbreaking work, we witness the birth of a new perspective on urban life—the sociospatial approach. Through its lens, we gain a deeper understanding of how social factors intersect with spatial arrangements to mold the city's fabric. From class divides to racial tensions, the city becomes a canvas upon which society paints its struggles and triumphs.

But amidst the chaos and complexity, a thread of hope emerges. Through our understanding of the sociospatial dynamic, we gain the power to shape the city's future—to build communities that reflect our values, aspirations, and dreams.

5

Walkable city

Walking is the oldest and simplest form of human transportation. Nowadays, walking a few blocks or crossing a street seems an inconvenience. Walkability is a new term to describe how friendly a city or a neighbourhood is too pedestrian activity. Walkable city considers persons, not their automobiles, at the center of the design scale.

How can we attract corporations, citizens, and mostly young, entrepreneurial talent? In Grand Rapids, Michigan, where the city's leading philanthropists employ me, they ask it differently: "How can we keep our children from leaving? How can we keep our grandchildren from leaving?"[35]

The metropolitan area that does not offer walkable urbanism is probably destined to lose economic development opportunities; the creative class will gravitate to those metro areas that offer multiple living arrangements. As consumer surveys in downtown Philadelphia and Detroit in 2006 have shown, this seems to be particularly true for the well-educated, who seem to prefer living in walkable urban places[36].

The obvious answer is that cities need to provide the sort of environment that these people want. Like many companies, an urban satellite is not enough. Brand Muscle, formerly of leafy Beachwood, Ohio, recently relocated all of its 150 employees to downtown Cleveland, thanks in part to a large twentysomething workforce's desires. Now staffer Kristen Babjack brags about her urban lifestyle to a restaurant to eat or go shopping. We have all of our arenas and sporting areas and concerts all in one pretty much walkable neighbourhood." Similar stories are making the news in Saint Louis, Buffalo, and even in beleaguered Detroit.

The economic advantage that has already begun to accrue to walkable places can be attributed to three key factors:

1. For specific segments of the population, chief among them young "creatives," urban living merely is more appealing; many wouldn't be caught dead anywhere else.
2. Massive demographic shifts occurring right now mean that these pro-urban segments of the population are becoming dominant, creating a spike in demand that is expected to last for decades.
3. The choice to live the walkable life generates considerable savings for these households, and much of these savings are spent locally.

The Economist magazine has its ranking that, although it uses. Mercer data tends to turn out a bit differently. It has been criticized as favouring Anglophone countries, which—although no help to the United States—means that eight of its top ten cities are in Canada, Australia, and New Zealand. But all are still places that are better for walking than driving.

Whomever you want to believe, the message is clear. Our cities, which are twice as efficient as our suburbs, burn twice the fuel of these European, Canadian, and Aussie/Kiwi places. Yet the quality of life in these foreign cities is deemed higher than ours, by a long shot. This is not to say that quality of life is directly related to sustainability, but merely that many Americans, by striving for a better experience, might find themselves moving to places that are more like the winners—or better yet, might try transforming their cities to resemble the winners.[37]

This sort of transformation could include many things, but one of them would undoubtedly be walkability. Vancouver, British Columbia, number one in The Economist's ranking, proves a useful model. By the mid-twentieth century, it was fairly indistinguishable from a typical U.S. city. Then, beginning in the late 1950s, when most American cities were building highways, Vancouver planners started to advocate for high-rise housing downtown.

This strategy, which included stringent requirements for green space and transit, really hit its stride in the mid-1990s, and the change has been profound. Since that time, the amount of walking and biking citywide has doubled, from 15 per cent to 30 per cent of all trips.

Vancouver is not ranked number one for livability because it is so sustainable; the things that make it bearable also make it livable.

Quality of life—which includes health and wealth—may not be a function of our ecological footprint, but the two are deeply interrelated. To wit, if we pollute so much because we are throwing away time, money, and lives on the highway, then both problems would seem to share a single solution, and that solution is to make our cities more walkable. Doing so is not easy, but it can be done, it has been done, and indeed it is being done in more than a few places at this very moment.[38]

If greater perceived danger leads to safer driving, how do you make the safest streets in the world? That question was probably best answered by Hans Monderman (1945–2008), the Dutch traffic engineer who pioneered two excellent and interrelated concepts: naked streets and shared space. While not appropriate everywhere, these techniques have a lot to teach us as we improve our cities. Bare streets refer to the concept of stripping a roadway of its signage —all of it, including stop signs, signals, and even stripes. Far from creating mayhem, this approach appears to have lowered crash rates wherever it has been tried. Following

Monderman's advice, the Danish town of Christiansfeld removed all signs and signals from its main intersection and watched the number of serious accidents each year fall from three to zero. The British county of Wiltshire, home to Stonehenge, pulled the centerline off a narrow street and witnessed a 35 per cent drop in the number of collisions.[39]

Drivers passed oncoming cars at a 40 per cent greater distance than on a striped street, even though the striped roadway was wider.

Monderman described his approach this way: "The trouble with traffic engineers is that when there's a problem with a road, they always try to add something. To my mind, it's much better to remove things."

This makes particular sense in the Netherlands, where there is a tradition of reticent roadways—you are unlikely to see a stop sign there—but the idea has also spread to Austria, France, Germany, Spain, and Sweden.[40]

Naked streets are also beginning to appear in the United States, typically in conjunction with Monderman's other big idea, shared space. In some ways, shared space is simply the extension of the naked streets' concept, including eliminating physical cues and barriers, such as curbs and distinct materials for roads and sidewalks. The goal is to create an environment of such utter ambiguity that cars, bicyclists, and pedestrians all come together in one big mixing bowl of humanity. As David Owen notes, "This sounds to many people like a formula for disaster." Not so: "The clear experience in the (mainly) European cities that have tried it has been that increasing the ambiguity of urban road spaces lowers car speeds, reduces accident rates, and improves the lives of pedestrians."[41]

In Monderman's terms, "Chaos equals cooperation."[42] In Monderman's terms, "Chaos eq Monderman was a man with the courage of his convictions. One of his favourite tricks with television reporters was to speak to them while standing in front of a shared-space intersection he had built in the Dutch village of Oosterwolde. Without missing a beat, he would blindly walk backwards into the flow of traffic, parting it like the Red Sea.

America has no shared-space examples as pure as Monderman's. Still, one of the first attempts can be found on Espanola Way in Miami Beach—just two blocks from the street that was unnecessarily widened a few pages ago. In good political fashion, the city asked the street's neighbours to participate in redesigning one of its key intersections, unaware that the neighbourhood was infested with urban designers just back from Europe. "No, curbs," we said. "Just pave it with bricks from building face to building face." Completed around 2000, Espanola Plaza works just fine, albeit with relatively low car counts. When the traffic engineers come to their senses, we will see Shared Streets begin to increase in the United States cooperation."

6

Industrial city

An industrial city is a zone or area that consists of a cluster of stand-alone industrial facilities, all operating simultaneously. It is usually located on the outskirts of a city and is normally provided with good transportation access, including road and rail.

Industrial cities or industrial towns refer to the city where the municipal economy and development are concentrated around industrial production and distinguished by many factories. The industrial city is at some stage during industrialization.

Industrialization affected many cities' internal structure, and by the end of nineteenth-century, the shape and functions of most cities and social relations appeared fundamentally changed. Manchester, England, is considered the archetype of the industrial city based on Friedrich Engels' observations.[43] Industrial cities might have had gone through the period featuring pollution. In the Chinese-speaking world, the term "industrial city" refers to cities in which heavy industries or the heavy industry leads the municipal economy a significant impression of the city to people other than its residents.[44]

Many people now spiking about post-industrialization.

Evans' analysis considers the scale and scope of the new economy clusters that have been favoured in these ostensible cities and regional strategic plans. The growth imperative is then discussed as it has been used to drive policy intervention and sectoral prioritisation of the creative economy.[45] This is manifested in both employment and GDP contribution to the city and national economies and the extent of 'creative class' presence in primarily central-city and city fringe (formerly industrial) areas. The creative sectors identified for support in these policy and investment plans are further analysed in terms of city cultural and economic prospects and wider economic development and cultural/policy strategies. A summary of intervention types is then discussed, including enterprise support, property- and area-based initiatives, common to many city plans, irrespective of their origin. An example of a 12-year creative industries policy programme is used to demonstrate the emphasis on startup and SMEs—using social regeneration and local economy rationales—at the cost of larger creative sectors which make up the dominant creative/knowledge economy and clusters, and which account for the growth performance which is claimed as the basis for further public-sector intervention.[46] The conclusion draws attention to the paradoxes and methodological issues that such policy analysis raises, notably the dependency on continued public intervention and subsidy in a new economy with such 'hope value' attached and given the creative industries' expansive spread its panacea status. In this sense, both *'cluster'* and *'growth'* theories and models are being applied without evidence to support their relevance or the scale at which they can be sustainable. This contrasts with the creative spaces that are the subject of regeneration, which are highly localised.

7

Creative city

The creative city has a diversified, sophisticated and internationally oriented cultural industries structure that nurtures and supports a wealth of local and international artistic activity that both are commercial, subsidised and voluntary.

The *creative city* is a concept developed by Australian David Yencken[47] in 1988 and has since become a global movement reflecting a new planning paradigm for cities. It was first described in his article *The Creative City*,[48] published in the literary journal Meanjin. In this article, Yencken argues that while cities must be efficient and fair, a creative city must also be committed to fostering creativity among its citizens and providing emotionally satisfying places and experiences for them.

The first mention of the creative city as a concept was in a seminar organized by the Australia Council, the City of Melbourne, the Ministry of Planning and Environment (Victoria) and the Ministry for the Arts (Victoria) in September 1988. Its focus was to explore how arts and cultural concerns could be better integrated into the planning process for city development. A keynote speech by David Yencken former Secretary for Planning and Environment for Victoria spelt out a broader agenda stating that while cities' efficiency is important, there is much more needed: "*The city should be emotionally satisfying and stimulate creativity amongst its citizens.*"⁴⁹ In subsequent writing about creative cities, the tendency has been to concentrate on one or other of the two necessary characteristics proposed by Yencken for a creative city but rarely on both together.

A significant follow-up initiative in Australia was a Creative Australia National Workshop in 1989 on '*The Relationship between Creativity and an Innovative Productive Future*' jointly sponsored by the Commission for the Future and the Australia Council for the Arts".

Another important early player was Comedia, founded in 1978 by Charles Landry. Its 1991 study, *Glasgow: The Creative City and its Cultural Economic*, was followed in 1994 by studying urban creativity called *The Creative City in Britain and Germany*.⁵⁰

The terms *cultural industries* and *cultural resources* were ints introduced into Europe by Franco Bianchini in 1990, who is coming from Italy was acquainted with their notion of *resorsi culturali* and further developed in Australia by Colin Mercer from 1991. Bianchini based his notions on Wolf von Eckhardt, who is 1980 in *The Arts & City Planning* noted that "effective cultural planning involves all the arts, the art of urban design, the art of winning community support, the art of transportation planning and mastering the dynamics of community development," to which Bianchini added "the art of forming partnerships between the public, private and voluntary sectors and ensuring the fair distribution of economic, social and cultural resources." Mercer added cultural planning has to be "the strategic and integral use of cultural resources in urban and community development." Bianchini elaborated the term cultural resource in collaborative work with Landry. They stated: "Cultural resources are the raw materials of the city and its value base; its assets replacing coal, steel or gold. Creativity is the method of exploiting these resources and helping them grow." This focus draws attention to the distinctive, the unique and the special in any place. This approach has been criticized by Jamie Peck as a "neoliberalizing" of a city's culture, as cultural spaces and elements are reconfigured into economic resources, thus bringing them inside the neoliberal market economy.[51]

As well as being centers of a creative economy and being home to a sizable creative class, creative cities have also been theorized to embody a particular structure. This structure comprises three categories of people, spaces, organizations, and institutions: the upper ground, the underground, and the middle ground.[52]

The upper ground consists of firms and businesses engaged in creative industries. These organizations create the economic growth one hopes to find in a creative city by taking the city's residents' creative product and converting it into a good or service that can be sold. The underground consists of the individual creative people—for example, artists, writers, or innovators—that produce this creative product. Then, the middle ground serves as a space for the upper ground and the underground to contact one another. The middle ground can consist of physical areas, for example, neighbourhoods with high populations of creative individuals, or galleries and bars where these individuals congregate. It can also consist of organizations, such as art collectives, that bring together creative individuals. The middle ground allows the underground creative product to be given a more concrete form by synthesizing disparate creative outputs into discrete products. Its capacity as space also allows individuals from the upper ground and individuals from the underground to meet, facilitating the transfer of ideas and people from one level to another.[53] The policy implications of this theoretical framework are that to harness the economic growth potential that creative industries bring with them, urban governments must foster the growth of the middle ground and underground and the upper ground. This can be done through urban planning initiatives that create spaces that can be used as a middle ground and encourage the "creative class" that comprises the underground.⁵⁴

Others have criticized this policy dimension of the creative city concept as a tool, not for revitalizing cities, but for creating an industry dedicated to offering urban renewal promises. In Richard Florida's work on creative cities and the creative class, he quantifies various city's "creative potential" measures. He then ranks cities based on his "creativity index". This, in turn, encourages cities to compete with one another for higher rankings and the attendant economic benefits that supposedly come with them. To do this, city governments will hire consulting firms to advise them on boosting their creative potential, creating an industry and a class of expertise centered around creative cities.⁵⁵

In the first years of the 21st century, the publication of John Howkin's *The Creative Economy* and Richard Florida's *The Rise of the Creative Class* gave the movement a dramatic lift as global restructuring was hitting deep into the US.⁵⁶ Florida's book hit a nerve with its clever slogans such as "talent, technology, tolerance" and interesting sounding indicators like the "bohemian index" or the "gay index", that gave numbers to ideas. Importantly it connected the three areas: a creative class – a novel idea, the creative economy and what conditions in cities attract the creative class. Florida concluded that economic development is driven largely by lifestyle factors, such as tolerance and diversity, urban infrastructure and entertainment.⁵⁷

Florida's work has been criticized by scholars such as Jamie Peck as, "work[ing] quietly with the grain of extant 'neoliberal' development agendas, framed around interurban competition, gentrification, middle-class consumption and place-marketing."⁵⁸ Florida's prescriptions favouring the city's fostering a creative class than being revolutionary are simply a way of bolstering the city's conventional economic model. The idea of the creative class serves to create a cultural hierarchy, and as such reproduce inequalities; indeed, even Florida himself has even acknowledged that the areas he himself touts as hotspots of the creative class are at the same time home to shocking disparities in economic status among their residents. To explain this, he points to the inflation of housing prices that an influx of creatives can bring to an area and the creative class' reliance on service industries that typically pay their employees' low wages.[59]

Critics also argue that the creative city idea has become a catch-all phrase in danger of losing its meaning. Cities also tend to restrict its meaning to the arts and activities within the creative economy professions, calling any cultural plan a creative city plan. Such activities are only one aspect of a community's creativity. There is a tendency for cities to adopt the term without thinking through their real organizational consequences and changing their mindset. The creativity implied in the term, the creative city, is about lateral and integrative thinking in all aspects of city planning and urban development, placing people, not infrastructure, at the centre of planning processes.

8

Consumer city

Economists define cities as the spatial concentration of economic actors. The concept is useful for understanding the development of urbanism in pre-industrial societies because it shows how large cities can develop without having the economic potential inside the city boundaries to sustain their own population. Thus, the concept allows escaping simplistic arguments that urbanisation in itself proves the sophistication, even the modernism of the city economy.

This basic viewpoint—that cities are good for production and bad for consumption— colors most of urban economics and has influenced most thinking on cities' future. The critical questions about the future of cities have always been

(1) *whether cities can maintain their productive edge in the world of information technology and speedy transportation,* and

(2) *whether the service industries that currently drive urban employment will stay in cities or follow manufacturing plants out to the non-city areas.*

That too little attention has been paid to the role of cities as centres of consumption. As human beings continue to get richer in the next century, quality of life will get increasingly critical in determining particular areas' attractiveness. After all, choosing a pleasant place to live is among the most natural ways to spend one's money. As Costa shows, between 1950 and 1990, the share of personal income in the United States spent on transportation and housing rose from 24 per cent to 35 per cent[60]. This increase can be seen as spending to get a desirable place to live. If these trends persist, then we must think that cities' future depends on particular urban areas' ability to provide attractive places for increasingly rich workers, who are less and less fettered by employment location constraints.[61]

The future of the city depends on the demand for density. If cities are going to survive and flourish, they must continue to want to live close to one another. Agglomeration effects—the effects of density—naturally determine the extent to which urban density is attractive. Most urban scholars think of cities as offering positive agglomeration benefits in the productive sphere, and as having negative agglomeration effects (or congestion effects) on non-work consumption. After all, firms and workers earn more in cities. In cities, workers pay higher rents, commute longer, and face more crime.[62]

The implications of this work for local governments, seeking to grow, seem clear. The sovereignty of the consumer is inescapable[63]. Trying to keep manufacturing is probably useless because of the negative amenities related to manufacturing possibly even harmful[64]. The key is to attract high human capital consumers. This means providing strong basic services like safe streets and good schools. As the desire for private schools continues to rise, it may be that allowing people who are paying for private schools to opt-out of a fraction of public school taxes may be a perfect means of attracting desirable urban residents. Naturally, policies that ensure an attractive city that is easy to get around will also be beneficial.

9

Green city

The green city is a city that promotes energy efficiency, and renewable energy in all its activities extensively promotes green solutions, applies land compactness with mixed land use and social mix practices in its planning systems, and anchors its local development in the principles of green growth and equity.

Urban green space, such as parks, forests, green roofs, streams, and community gardens, provides critical ecosystem services. Green space also promotes physical activity, psychological well-being, and the general public health of urban residents.

What is a Green City? "Chicago" represents the greater metropolitan area surrounding the city of Chicago. A metropolitan area is a core area containing a substantial population nucleus, together with adjacent communities having a high degree of social and economic integration with that core. Metropolitan areas can comprise one or more entire counties.[65]

Focusing on metropolitan areas makes sense because, in the United States, most people and jobs are now located within metropolitan areas but outside central cities.[66] Defining greenness is a tougher task. Many of us have an intuitive sense of what sets a green city, such as Portland, Oregon, apart from brown urban centers, like Mexico City. Green cities have clean air and water and pleasant streets and parks. Green cities are resilient in the face of natural disasters, and the risk of major infectious disease outbreaks in such cities is low. Green cities also encourage green behaviour, such as public transit, and their ecological impact is relatively small. Public health experts focus on the health consequences of exposure to local air pollutants, dirty water, and other environmental factors that promote disease. According to Khan, a city is considered green if environmentally linked diseases are relatively low. Finally, many economists evaluate the urban environment by examining differences in real estate prices across cities at a point in time or for the same city over time. If home prices are much higher in San Francisco than in Detroit, this suggests that people prefer to live in San Francisco—in part because of its superior environmental quality.[67] How does growth affect a city's prospects for becoming more—or less— green? Khan's book takes the first cut at this problem by providing an overview of the environmental Kuznets curve[68], including a discussion of its history and some examples of environmental indicators that follow the EKC pattern—that is, first deteriorating and then improving as per capita income grows.[69] This chapter briefly describes the main channels through which income growth affects environmental quality and several key factors that can alter the EKC's shape (environmental Kuznets curve). Also, it presents several limitations to the hypothesis, including concerns raised by environmentalists.

10

Healthy City

A healthy city is not one that has achieved a particular health status. · It is conscious of health and striving to improve it. A healthy city is continually creating and improving those physical and social environments and expanding those community resources that enable people to mutually support each other in performing all the functions of life and developing to their maximum potential.

In the 1820s, French epidemiologist *Louis René Villermé* noted that the wealthier the Parisian neighbourhood, or arrondissement, the lower was the mortality rate and likelihood of illness. By 1842, Edwin Chadwick had built on Villermé's work. He published the Report on the Sanitary Conditions of the Labouring Population in Great Britain, documenting that the 'gentry and professional' classes lived longer than 'labourers and artisans.'[70] Miasma—filth or dirty air—was the leading theory of disease causation. Sanitary commissions were created in European and American cities to clean up urban environments with the hope of arresting infectious disease epidemics. [71]

Sanitary engineers tended to address urban health issues by employing new technologies to remove waste by, for instance, piping it away from cities into rivers and oceans (Melosi 2000). When removing the miasma did not seem to reduce disease, the sick were removed from society. Contagion, the belief in the direct passage of poison from one person to another, led to many immigrants' large quarantines and justified state-sponsored interventions in the economy.[72]

School enrolment rates are in general higher in cities than in villages. The largest cities' financial strength likewise opens up opportunities for diversification in culture, the arts and science, accompanied by technological innovation. This illustrates the strong link in megacities between economic opportunities and the development of social and human capital. A third opportunity (and another scale effect) can satisfy human energy and material requirements in a cost-effective and ecologically oriented way. It points to the argument referring to economies of scale mentioned above but takes it a step further by addressing energy and resource aspects. The population's concentration potentially reduces the per capita demand for occupied land, the cost of providing treated water or collecting solid and liquid waste. It also permits implementation of mass transit facilities, reducing the demand for private vehicles in the process. Several 'visible' examples of mobility demonstrate the potential of 'marrying economic and ecological goals'. In 2003, the city of London introduced a tax on each vehicle entering the city centre. As a result, the traffic volume decreased by 15%, and drivers spent 30% less time traffic congestion.[73]

Megacities, however, are likewise spaces of risk. Most of the world's largest cities are concentrated in areas where natural hazards such as earthquakes, floods and landslides are likely to happen.[74] Consequently, the number of losses (lives and values lost) also increased (International Federation 1 Introduction: Megacities in Latin America as Risk Habitat 7 of Red Cross and Red Crescent Societies 2010). This does not imply that megacities are particularly threatened or have a monopoly on risk. Due to the concentration of people and values in hazardous locations, i.e., flood or earthquake zones, however, the extent of a potential risk event is estimated to exceed the capacity of a megacity to react, with the consequence of, particularly high losses. Apart from natural hazards, there are human-made (environmental and technological) risks. The rapid change in land use often exacerbates the risk of floods, while interference with water catchments jeopardizes the water supply's quality and quantity. Flood risk is, therefore, a good example of the close link between natural hazards and human-made risks. Other examples of human-made risks are uncontrolled waste disposal leading to environmental degradation and health risks to urban dwellers (particularly those living in precarious locations), system leakages, industrial and toxic waste resulting in ground-water pollution. Large quantities of untreated sewage curtail water downstream and mounting traffic substantially to worsening air quality and health risks such as respiratory disease. The rapid increase in energy consumption outpaces the energy system's capacity in place and threatens energy security in the long run. Socio-spatial segregation in cities and disparities between affluent gated communities, on the one hand, and informal neighbourhoods, on the other hand, bear risks of a widening social divide, violence and crime. While this portfolio of risks may appear diverse, the risks themselves have two elements in common. The first of all confirm that although large agglomerations face numerous risks, on the other hand, they produce and reinforce them.

Pelling also states that "urbanization affects disasters just as profoundly as disasters affect urbanization."[75] Secondly, vulnerability to the dangers associated with environmental degradation, poor housing and sanitation or the lack of access to basic services differs significantly across locations and social groups. People in slums suffer on average, more detrimental health outcomes and are more vulnerable to floods. Women, children and the elderly are the most vulnerable of all.[76] The occurrence of natural and human-made risks cannot be treated as two separate entities. Rather, the natural dimension is inextricably bound up with the human or social dimension. Flood risk, for example, may depend on the likelihood of a hazardous rainfall event (as a natural cause) but is largely triggered by human action, such as settlement construction in hazard-prone areas, which can lead to functional changes in the natural system and impede the mitigation of flood extremes. The considerations of megacities as spaces of risk related to the notion of risk and vulnerability. These aspects will be taken up in the following section, and the underlying risk definitions and concepts briefly addressed. The intention is not to cover the entire risk debate found in the literature.

11

Megacity

The term "megacity" refers to metropolitan areas with a total population of more than 10 million people.

Historically rapid urbanization has its roots in today's more developed regions. According to the United Nations (2008), the world's urban share rose from around 3% in 1900 to one-third in the early 1950s, reaching 50% in 2008. Predictions suggest that this trend will continue. Urban population growth of about 1.7% per annum will bring the number of urban dwellers worldwide from currently 3.5 billion to roughly 5 billion by 2030, increasing corresponding to creating a city with approximately 1.5 million inhabitants every 10 days.[77]

The world's urban population is distributed among settlements of different sizes along a continuum from small towns with several thousand people to giant cities with populations of tens of millions. Most of the urban population live in settlements with fewer than 500,000 inhabitants. Most of these intermediate settlements function as links between town and country where agricultural surpluses are exchanged for manufactured goods and services following central place theory precepts.[78]

By 1990 twelve cities had attained this size and shared 7.1 per cent of the world urban population. It is anticipated that by 2015 twenty-seven cities will reach the 10 million mark, accommodating 10.9 per cent of the world urban population. In absolute numerical terms, this represents a rise from 12 million people living in a single city in 1950 to 450 million in several giant cities by 2015. Between 1990 and 2015, nearly all the population growth in the largest urban agglomerations is expected to occur in the LDRs. At the other end of the population-size continuum, cities with fewer than 500,000 inhabitants were home to 63.7 per cent of the world urban population in 1950. In contrast, their share is expected to decrease.

One of the most striking features of the global urban pattern is how the urban population lives in giant cities that dominate the global urban and economic systems. Against the background of a general increase in the number of people living in urban places, metropolitan regions proliferate and expand rapidly.[79]

Although urbanization is a global phenomenon, it does not occur as a homogeneous process across regions and countries, or even within one country. The overwhelming majority of the population of Europe (72%) and North America (80%) now lives in towns and cities. Among the developing world regions, it is the region of Latin America and the Caribbean, with its exceptionally high urbanisation level (around 78%), that ranks as advanced in this context. In contrast, most people in the continents of Africa and Asia still live in rural areas (approx. 60%). Urbanization levels are expected to rise in the coming decades, particularly in the developing world (UN Population Division 2007, 2008). The emergence of the megacity is perhaps the most visible expression of the mega-trend urbanization. There is some consensus on the definition of megacities as urban agglomerations of at least ten million inhabitants.[80] The number increased dramatically from three megacities (Mexico City, New York, Tokyo) in 1975 to around

20 in 2007 and is projected to reach almost 30 worldwide by 2025. The group of emerging megacities whose populations range from five to ten million have likewise experienced a notable increase. The number is expected to increase from currently about 30 to almost 50 in 2025. Together, 'established' and emerging megacities now account for roughly 15% of the world's total urban population.[81] This share is predicted to increase to approximately 17% by 2025. The largest urban agglomerations are not necessarily those with the fastest population growth. A third of the current megacities with more than ten million inhabitants report a population increase of less than 1.5% for 1975–2007. In Tokyo, for example, the growth rate was slightly less than 1% and is predicted to decline further up to 2025. On the other hand, cities like Karachi (3.5%), Dhaka (5.6%) and Bogotá (3.5%) have witnessed extremely rapid growth. Even where proportional rates seem low, the absolute population figures continue to rise significantly. The current 1.8% population growth rate for Mexico City, for example, still adds approximately 400,000 people to its urban population every year. At an approximate growth rate of 2% population doubles every 35 years, at a growth rate of 3%, it doubles every 17 years. Following these figures, the primary and perhaps most defining attribute of the megacity is its magnitude in terms of population. Megacities and their urban populations have reached incomparable scales. Not only are they larger in terms of population than ever before, but also terms of physical extent, environmental impact, values and economic importance. They are 'global cities' in a global economy or 'primate' cities with a prominent role in their respective countries.[82]

A second defining feature of the megacity is the speed of change. It took just 50 years for Dhaka, for example, to advance from a population of less than 1 to currently almost 15 million. As populations grow, urban land expands to provide accommodation and services. While most of history, the rate of urban land expansion was low and physical boundaries shifted at moderate rates, contemporary land conversion occurs rapidly. Changes in lifestyle, housing demands and mobility, and socio-economic change are key factors behind this development. A third distinguishing characteristic of the megacity is its complexity[83]. The rapid change and unprecedented scale of populations and physical expansion that characterize mega-urbanization sets the stage for highly complex simultaneous and interactive processes.

Megacities are, for example, embedded in complex global-local relationships. Their emergence and development is both a trend and an expression of globalization, with intense interdependencies regarding the exchange of information, goods and the use of resources[84]. Global dimensions are intrinsic to megacities since resources have a decisive impact on resource regimes and ecosystems worldwide. On the other hand, environmental change, and more specifically, climate change, impacts back on megacities. In this sense, they are culprits and victims of global change at the same time.[85] Megacities also prove complex concerning governance structures. Mexico City is an illustrative case. The metropolitan region is divided into four main administrative units: the federal district (which itself is subdivided into 16 units), the administration of the state of Mexico and Hidalgo (with 59 municipal administrations) and the national government ministries with key responsibilities in the operation of various sectors[86]. Interaction between government rules and spontaneous, decentralized decisions renders this complexity more acute. The provision of basic services such as water, shelter and mobility serves as an example. In many megacities, it is organized by a huge variety of decentralized individual and informal institutions outside the formal set of rules, particularly when governments fail or are unable to ensure the provision of basic goods and services.[87]

Unprecedented scale, rapid change, and complexity define the characteristics that transform the urban habitat into a space of opportunity and risk space. Megacities provide first and foremost economic opportunities.[88] They are engines of global economic growth and contribute more than proportionately to the national output. As an illustration, approximately half of the world's megacities generate more than a third of their respective countries' gross domestic product (GDP).[89] Cities like Bangkok or Sao Paulo are home to between 10% and 15% of the national population but contribute more than 40% to the GDP. These high relative productivity levels are attributed to large agglomerations' scale advantages in providing public and private goods and more favourable specialisation conditions.[90] This associate with the network and cluster effects of economic branches that lead to further efficiency gains. Key to this development is the opening of national economies, promoting the mobilization of goods, capital and people, and an international division of labour. These tendencies are not expected to change in the future and may even intensify due to increased globalization. Closely related to economic opportunities is the potential for social and human capital. Education (from pre-school to university) is more advanced in large agglomerations than in smaller cities and rural areas.

12

Charter city

A charter city is a city where the governing system is defined by the city's own charter document rather than by general law.

According to Paul Romer: The two most exciting precedents for Charter Cities are Hong Kong and Shenzhen, so it has some origins. They each played essential roles in fostering reform of the Chinese economy. But it is an approach that can be used in any country that wants to implement reforms, even a developed country like the United States. It turns out that this is a unique time in human history when it is possible to start many new cities because there is an enormous, unmet demand for city life.[91]

What are the essential elements of a Charter City?

Based on Romer, the essence of the idea is the notion of a Startup City. You have a chance to start a city new. Then the question is: "What can you accomplish with that? What are the things that will be required to make it successful?" I think what is unusual about a Startup City, as opposed to an existing city, is that you can propose something new without having to go through a long process of consultation and agreement amongst the people that might be affected by a change, one that would inevitably mean that a change that some people do not want is imposed on them.[92]

With a Startup City, you can propose something entirely new and let people choose whether they want to live under its rules, as embodied in its charter, the document that specifies its founding principles. People who want to try the reform can go there, and people who don't, they don't have to. With a startup, you can have reform without coercion.

This is part of the insight that Deng Xiaoping had in pursuing Shenzhen. As he explained later, he wanted a way to open the Chinese economy that avoided long argument and contention about what types of change to pursue and how to pursue them.

The idea is also closely related to a special zone concept, but it is a specific type of special area.

First, a Charter City has to be significant. Viable cities will have millions of residents, so a zone has to be big to accommodate them. Second, it should be a Reform Zone, not a Concession Zone. Most zones are created to offer concessions to firms, not to implement reforms. The goal of a Charter City is reform, not giving out privileges, so in this sense, the motivation for a Charter City is different from the reason behind most special zones.[93]

Here are two tests for whether a policy is a reform or a concession: Would you be happy if this policy lasts forever? Would you be pleased if this policy spread to the entire country? If the answer to both questions is yes, it is a reform. If not, it is almost indeed a concession, a gift to some particular interest. A reform zone is a zone that implements one or more fundamental reforms.[94]

So to summarize, a Charter City is a city-scale reform zone where a startup city could emerge.

13

Startup city

Startup Cities as the venue for identity formation and social capital benefit. Geographically discrete transnational social spaces let group members trade on shared values and expertise. Community membership defined by similar outlook, values and approach rather than shared nationality. Allow entrepreneurs to bridge structural holes in their networks, bestowing legitimacy Startup cities allow startuppers to engage in identity formation practices of learning, sharing, teaching.

Does it matter where startups locate? Issues of the location to startups because the people who provide them with the resources they need to grow—revenues, talent, capital, advice—are more than producers of code or PowerPoint decks. They live in houses or apartments and commute to offices.[95] They attend meetings and bump into each other randomly at coffee shops and in hallways. And company founders seeking to build, develop, and sustain vital trust relationships with their startup's customers, suppliers, employees, mentors, and investors must repeatedly meet people in person. Startups thrive or fizzle depending on the quality of these people and the strength of those relationships. And part of that quality depends on where a startup locates.[96]

Pick the right one, and the startup gets the resources that it needs to grow. Pick the wrong place to run the company, and it withers in the struggle to get those resources.

It is essential to distinguish between a company founded to support its CEO and staff and companies funded by venture capital firms seeking rapid growth that culminates in an initial public offering or acquisition. Jan Rivkin, Harvard Business School Bruce V. Rauner Professor of Business Administration, pointed out that this statement is not precisely correct because it depends on defining a startup. If a startup is a small, private company, such as a restaurant, that is intended to help a founder and its employees to make a living. Such startups are widely distributed geographically.

However, if a startup is thought of as a small private company whose goal is to get big fast, whose investors hope to get more prosperous when the company is acquired or goes public, then startups are concentrated. The Kauffman Foundation refers to such fast-growing startups as gazelles, emphasizing that such startups are distinguished by their ability to overgrow while developing new products, winning customers, and delivering a high service level. Kauffman argued that gazelles account for 50% of new jobs, expand into new geographies, and create growth in related industries.

Gazelles concentrate in specific locations because of the overwhelming advantages that those locations provide to entrepreneurs and investors. Rivkin suggested that gazelles have good reasons to locate in a relatively small number of specific cities such as Boston, Silicon Valley, and Los Angeles. As he said, "Venture capital is spiky. The top 50 metro areas receive 97% of the venture capital. 83% of the venture capital investment goes to places like San Francisco, Boston, and Southern California." Such concentration happens because it works. "It goes back to Alfred Marshall in the 1890s.[97] Agglomeration happens for a reason: positive feedback loops between skilled labour and specialized inputs such as venture capital. Computer scientists want to be in the Bay Area; biotechnologists flock to Boston and Cambridge; media people go to New York. As Marshall wrote, 'Mysteries are as if they were in the air,'" explained Rivkin. And while universities are often a starting point for a booming startup region, its talent network's magnetic power can overcome the economic barriers imposed by high housing costs, congestion, and exhausting commutes.[98]

Stanford Business School Fred H. Merrill Professor of Economics Paul Oyer explained "it is almost impossible for cities that attempt to make themselves into the next Silicon Valley. [Startup cities] get started thanks to research and education. Towns with noted universities like Silicon Valley, Research Triangle Park, and Austin get people who graduate, live there, and get together. The network is valuable." Oyer points out that universities are a necessary but not sufficient condition. "If universities alone were all that was needed, Missoula, Mont., where the University of Montana is located, would be a startup hub. It would be best if you also had companies. For example, Stanford had Hewlett Packard and Schlumberger." Oyer sees many factors that could, but don't destroy Silicon Valley as a startup hub. "It is hard for other cities to break in because of the power of the network that gets created, which grows as each new person comes here.

And venture capitalists want to be where the talent is.[99] The strength of the network overwhelms all the factors that should kill Silicon Valley, such as the high cost of living and high tax rates," he explained. These regions are irresistible to entrepreneurs because they enable gazelles to raise capital and hire talent in large enough blocks to get big fast. As Harvard Business School Professor of Management Practice Shikhar Ghosh said, "A company like Facebook, which is trying to get big fast, can get the resources it needs in Boston when it's small, but if it wants to get big, it needs to move to a place like Silicon Valley where it can more easily raise the capital it needs in big increments. A company that ultimately wants to employ 20,000 to 30,000 people will move to an area that has the capital to help it raise Series B, C, and D funding."

Another critical resource that gazelles need to hire in big chunks is talented people. George Foster, Konosuke Matsushita Professor of Management at the Stanford Graduate School of Business, said "In Silicon Valley, an entrepreneur Startup Cities 13 hires 500 software engineers quickly. And China is becoming another such place. It produces 200,000 engineers a year, and 2,000 of them are truly great." If talent is concentrated in a specific region, the risk of working for a startup declines substantially. Over the last five to 10 years, an exciting development has been moving that talent into cities, thus replotting the centre of gravity for Silicon Valley to San Francisco and Massachusetts's Route 128 to Boston and Cambridge.

Harvard Business School Associate Professor William Kerr explained, "Culture favours some places over others. People want to be in places where everyone idolizes entrepreneurs. They want to be where you can try and fail and not be ostracized. In the Boston area, young talent wants to live in cities, which is making it hard for me to find a buyer for my three-acre property in [the upscale, rural suburb 25 miles from Boston] Lincoln." Startup-rich regions such as Silicon Valley and Cambridge achieved their status as world leaders over many decades. In looking back over those decades, experts note that the initial spark for their emergence as leaders was the presence of outstanding leaders who started successful companies close to universities with startup-friendly values. These startups grew, went public, and became local pillars.[100]

New companies spun off from these pillars attracted new capital and fresh talent eager to partake in similar startup success. Before getting into how they evolved, it is worth noting that MIT and Stanford have created a tremendous amount of wealth. Lesley reported that by 2014 MIT alumni had created 30,200 companies with $1.9 trillion in revenue, which employed 4.6 million people. Stanford had done even more: by

2011 Stanford alumni had created 39,900 companies with $2.7 trillion in revenue and 5.4 million jobs. As mentioned earlier, great leaders spurred the emergence of Silicon Valley and Cambridge. For example, as MIT Sloan School Lecturer Jorge Guzman pointed out, Silicon Valley would still be peach orchards were not for William Shockley, the transistor's inventor. The latter moved west to found Fairchild Semiconductor.

MIT Sloan School David Sarnoff Professor of Management of Technology Ed Roberts noted that Frederick Terman, an MIT professor who came to Stanford and helped two of his students, William Hewlett and David Packard, helped HP help HP succeed by connecting the company to Defense Department contracts. In Cambridge, there likely would be no venture capital industry were it not for Harvard Business School professor Georges Doriot and MIT alum Ken Olson. They founded Digital Equipment Corp. with funds from Doriot's American Research and Development. As MIT Professor of Technological Innovation, Entrepreneurship, and Strategic Management James Utterback explained, "From a 50-year career perspective, the key to the success of Cambridge and Silicon Valley is leadership within a context."[101] So, What Is Startup Common? As Utterback implied, great leaders can't build companies all by themselves. For that, they need talent and fresh ideas that come from local universities. As Roberts pointed out, MIT was started in 1861 with the motto Mens et Manus (Latin for mind and hand), meaning that its mission was to make cutting edge ideas useful to industry. What's more, MIT encouraged professors to research the sector to supplement their low professors' pay. Thus, there was a natural flow of talent between MIT and industry, which is frowned on in other universities. Capital, talent, and pillar companies follow initial startup success.[102] Venture capitalists are pack animals; if they see that another firm has profited through investment, they will seek similar ones. So an initial success will attract more capital, and venture capitalists will create a snowball effect if that new capital is thriving. If some startups go public and scale, they become pillar companies that reinvest their wealth and talent in the region. And that local success attracts more people in the local universities to go into startups.

The most important factors that cause scale-up are opportunity and people. But there is a debate over whether the best talent will find the biggest opportunity.[103] As these experts explained, the emergence of a local startup hub takes decades. The Startup Common is different because it provides a way to explain how overtime specific regions may rise and fall based on the relative strength or weakness of the six startup common elements. What makes the startup Common valuable is that it integrates all the components into one model that can help leaders explain where a region is now, the vision for its success as a startup hub, and point the way to closing the gap.

14

Smart city

A smart city is a municipality that uses information and communication technologies to increase operational efficiency, share information with the public and improve both the quality of government services and citizen welfare.

The label smart city has been spreading worldwide, impacting urban strategies in both large and small towns. To face the increasing problems of urban areas, local public government, companies, not for profit organizations and the citizens themselves embraced the idea of a smarter city, using more technologies, creating better living conditions and safeguarding the environment. However, today the smart city panorama appears very confused. No acknowledged smart city definition exists till now and several cities defining themselves smart completely lack a strategic vision about their smart future.[104] This part aims to offer a large vision about the smart city phenomenon and to compare researches and considerations regarding how to define a smart city, how to design a smart strategy and how to measure if smart actions really can create public value for citizens and a better quality of life in urban spaces.[105]

Cities whose economic-development strategy is a corporate-capture strategy are typically those whose economic development director and planning director don't talk to each other.

Like Lowell, the smart cities hire a director of planning and development, who is first charged with creating a city where people want to be. Rather than land new office tenants in a shrinking office market, this person understands that future economic growth will occur where the creative people are, and then works to lure more residents downtown.[106]

As Adam Baacke suggested, this strategy means building more market-rate housing while also promoting those things that residents want and need: parks and playgrounds, supermarkets and farmers' markets, cafés and restaurants—and, eventually, good schools—all embraced in a framework of top-notch walkability. Each of these items is a book in its own right, and well beyond this discussion. Suffice it to say that they are necessary and that the first step to attracting them is to reorient economic development around creating a downtown that has them all.[107] However, the smart city idea has more ancient roots.[108] A large literature survey about smart city and digital city scientific papers, realized by Annalisa Cocchia.[109] Therefore, the idea of a smart and digital city, that is, to use technology and especially ICT to improve the quality of life in urban space, is quite old.[110]

But only during the latest years, the attention of this topic has a peek. There are several reasons about this evidence: the larger diffusion of mobile devices and the Internet among citizens, the higher and higher dimensions of cities, the need to safeguard the environment from pollution and energy consumption.[111] Today smart city is in the mood, not only in academic or scientific research but also in public government choices and projects. Looking for smart city web sites, the results are millions. It seems that every city worldwide, across continents and independently from dimension, culture, economic situation, considers important to be smart. For these reasons, the panorama is very confused.[112]

A deeper analysis of the literature survey, presented by Cocchia and also by Dameri in their work *"Smart and Digital City: A Systematic Literature Review,"* considering not only the number of papers or their geographical distribution but also their content, shows that a shared and sound definition of the smart city still lacks.[113] Even if there are some most cited definitions, their meaning is quite different from each other. Moreover, owing to the continuous and fast innovation regarding the smart city enabling technologies, it is difficult to compare definitions written in a time elapse of three/four years.[114]

Also, the smart city empirical implementation shows the same heterogeneity. Cities have been starting to implement their own smart projects. Both citizens, companies and public governments have very high expectations from the positive impact of smart actions on the quality of life or their city's appeal. Sometimes a smart city project is seen as a panacea able to solve all the urban problems, such as pollution, local public transport difficulties, inequalities between people, economic crisis, etc. But these expectations are often not supported nor by a clear smart vision of the city nor by effective smart programs and initiatives.[115]

The smart city implementation generally rises like a bottom-up phenomenon. Several actors independently start to realize a smart initiative, using some public infrastructures or technological solutions. For example, a public hospital realizes on-line health record access. A company supplies electric cars to its employers, and the municipality replaces old buses with new ones, with a lower impact on air pollution. Three smart actions, using technology to improve the quality of life in urban spaces and reduce pollution and energy consumption, but not included into a comprehensive vision can define goals, expected results, and scheduled time for project realization. Moreover, the lack of a framework to collect all these initiatives prevents them from implementing important synergies and communicating to the citizens of the city's improved smartness.[116] The technology is certainly the core aspect of a smart city, but it is not enough to create public value for citizens. The human contribution is necessary to embody smart actions into people living, studying, working in the city or visiting the city for one or a few days for work or tourism.

Therefore, it should be necessary to speak about smart people in smart city and consider people, technology, and strategic vision like indispensable components of a successful smart program. The lack of a smart strategic vision negatively impacts the performance obtained by smart projects and initiatives. Moreover, no city has developed and applied key performance indicators and a measurement framework to evaluate smart actions' real effectiveness.[117]

Perhaps it is not severe when the smart city is a pioneering project. Still, it becomes a real obstacle in obtaining success when the smart city project wants to deliver sustainable returns to large public and private investments.[118]

The mosaic emerging from the smart city panorama is colorful and rich in suggestions to support further studies and better implementation plans. It clearly emerges that a smart city is a complex challenge because it involves several dimensions: technology, citizens, public and private bodies, urban vision. Moreover, it interests cities all over the world, with very great differences from each other: cultural, economic, social.[119]

Each city wants both to apply a shared smart city idea and to pursue its own specific goals. This complexity requires the development of a governance framework of smart cities, built upon a shared smart city definition, but flexible to be adapted to different and specific needs; it should include all the steps of the governance activity, that is: to define a strategic vision, to design long term strategies, to prioritize and schedule projects and to measure the obtained results for different stakeholders.

Why is it so difficult to define a smart city? There are several reasons.

As Cocchia and Dameri show in their book, the emerging of smart themes is originally strictly joined with the digital city idea. Indeed, examining the most cited definitions of smart city and digital city listed by Cocchia in the next chapter, several elements are the same in both the topics. But an important reason to explain the difficult to define the smart city should be found in its bottom-up nature. Rising from the empirical application, the concrete smart city is especially a collection of several projects, initiatives, and public and private actions.

Therefore, as these initiatives result from R. P. Dameri and C. Rosenthal-Sabroux spontaneous choices by different actors, depending on their own interests and the specificity of a city, the collections are very heterogeneous. To design a definition observing one or several case studies means writing a definition describing a specific smart city, not a standard.[120]

Giffinger, one of the most-cited authors in the smart city field of study, also examines the different topics involved in the smart city implementation.[121] Certainly, all these themes are included in smart cities, but not in each smart city, and not only these themes are included. Moreover, some of these themes sometimes overlap each other, and the clearness of the Giffinger's definition is not satisfying. It says: *"A Smart City is a city well performing built on the 'smart' combination of endowments and activities of self-decisive, independent and aware citizens".*[122]

This definition is broad enough to include all the good initiatives carried out to improve the city quality, no matters which instruments, outcomes or actors are involved.

This definition could be interesting for a theoretical debate about what a smart city is. Still, it is not very useful to drive its implementation and to measure the obtained results. As listed in the chapter written by Cocchia, examining other smart city definitions emerges a large disagreement between the academic view and the empirical view about smart cities. This disagreement regards the main component of a smart city: in the academic debate, it is the intellectual capital, in the empirical vision expressed by large companies such as IBM, Cisco and so on, the main component is the technology.

This different vision impacts all the smart city's further aspects: strategy definition, implementation, evaluation and performance measurement. The academic vision considers the intellectual capital the most important resource to increase the smartness of a city.[123]

The label intellectual capital is to be interpreted in the broader meaning. It includes the culture of citizens, their educational level, their intellectual capability; but also the culture of companies, that is, trademarks, patents, know-how, reputation on the market; and finally the city culture, represented by museums, theatres, cinemas, cultural events and everything could animate the cultural life in the city.[124]

Depending on this vision, the smarter city is the one that has, the larger cultural capital and can use its knowledge to choose the better solutions for the further development of the city quality. Therefore, investments in cultural initiatives are welcome, but the city should use its awareness to promote sustainable development, equal economic growth, and environmental quality in urban areas.[125] Also, the evaluation system is consequently designed depending on this intangible vision. Indicators regarding the city's cultural aspect, the citizens and the public and private bodies resident in the city are the main proxy of the city smartness. To increase the cultural level—and in this way, the smartness—of the city is the main instrument to attract further the best people and companies: more educated, more innovative, more profitable.[126]

A smart city's business vision is strongly based on technology's pivotal role, especially ICT. It derives from both the previous idea of digital city and the strong need to solve several concrete problems strongly affecting the life Smart City and Value Creation 5 in a large metropolis, such as traffic, pollution, energy consumption, and waste treatment, water quality. These aspects are also near the idea that green cities and environmental themes are an important part of smart city goals. In this smart city vision, initiatives to improve the city smartness are especially focused on some lines such as:

- energy production from renewable sources, to reduce energy cost, CO_2 emissions and to satisfy the increasing energy demand in urban areas;
- building efficiency to reduce energy demand and consumption;
- local transport quality and greenness, to reduce pollution deriving from transport in cities;
- and so on. The evaluation system applied to this different smart city vision is more tangible and based on physic indicators such as CO_2 emissions, greenhouse gases, waste tons, megawatts produced by renewable sources, etc.

It is important to outline that, even if the ultimate goal is to improve the citizens' quality of life, they are scarcely considered in this smart city vision, and smart initiatives are often planned without their involvement. They are seen like the smart city value chain's final addresser, but this value is not compared with their own expectations about their quality of life. Even if these two smart city visions are quite clear in academic papers and empirical studies or surveys about smart cities, they are scarcely applied when a smart city plan is designed.[127]

As Thorne and Griffith explain in their chapter about the London Smart City development, and as it emerges from several authors' large literature surveys, the different smart city souls are merged. They are not able to distinguish themselves in a smart strategy.[128] Technological, cultural and environmental aspects are the core elements of a smart city. Still, their role is not the same. It is important to explicitly declare which aspect is the most important, what has the leading role, and how this component interacts with the smart city strategy's main stakeholders, that is, the citizens. To explicitly define the smart city vision and align it with smart initiatives and desired outcomes is the first step to implementing a successful smart city program.

15

Happy city

The happy city is a concept that treats emotional infrastructure as the most important infrastructure in any city. Cities are the collection of people and infrastructure; however, if there is a well-developed system for ensuring well-being, comfort, exchange of ideas and thoughts, thereby creating a healthy emotional.

Suppose one was to judge by sheer wealth. In that case, the last half-century should have been an ecstatically happy time for people in the United States and other wealthy nations such as Canada, Japan, and Great Britain. Riches were piled upon means. By the turn of the century, Americans travelled having their own detached home. The stock of cars—and bedrooms and toilets—far surpassed the number of humans who used them.[129] It was an age of unprecedented bounty and growth, at least until the great recession of 2008 stuck a needle into the balloon of optimism and easy credit. And yet the boom decades of the late twentieth century were not accompanied by a boom in happiness. Surveys show that people's assessment of their well-being in the United States pretty much flatlined during that time.[130]

So, it was the same as citizens in Japan and the United Kingdom.

Canada fared only slightly better. China, the new star of supercharged GDP growth, is providing yet more evidence of a paradox. Between 1999 and 2010, a decade in which average purchasing power in China grew more than threefold, people's ratings of their life satisfaction stalled, according to Gallup polls (although urbanized Chinese were happier than their rural cousins). In the final decades of the last century, Americans increasingly complained of personal problems.[131]

By 2005 clinical depression was three to ten times as common as it was two generations ago. By 2010, one in ten Americans reported that they suffered from depression. Six to eight times as many college students experienced depression in 2007 as they did in 1938. Although this may be partly due to cultural factors—it's now more acceptable to talk about depression—objective mental health statistics are not encouraging. High school and college students—the most comfortable group to survey—climbed higher and higher on mental health researchers cheerily call the Paranoia, Hysteria, Hypochondriasis, and Depression scales.[132]

One in ten Americans is taking antidepressants. Analysis from free-market think tanks such as the Cato Institute assures us that *"high levels of economic freedom and high average incomes are among the strongest correlates of subjective well-being,"* which is to say that being rich and free should make us happier. So why wasn't the half-century surge in wealth accompanied by a rise in happiness?

What was counteracting the effect of all that money? Some psychologists point to the phenomenon dubbed the *"hedonic treadmill"*: the natural human tendency to shift our expectations along with our changing fortunes. The treadmill theory suggests that the richer you get, the more you compare yourself to other rich people and the faster the wheel of desire spins beneath your feet so that you end up feeling as though you haven't made any progress. Others blame the growing income gap and the realization by millions of middle-class Americans that they were falling farther behind society's wealthiest members, especially during the last two decades.[133]

There is some explanatory truth in both of these theories. However, economists have crunched the survey numbers and concluded that they only partially explain the widening gap between material and emotional wealth. The decades-long expansion in the American economy paralleled society's migration from the country to cities and cities to the sprawl's in-between world. Since 1940, almost all urban growth has been suburban. In the decade before the big bust of 2008, the economy was driven largely by the boundless culdesac, tract housing, and big-box power centring of the urban fringe landscape. For a time, it was impossible to separate growth from suburbanization.

They were the same thing. More people than ever got precisely what they thought they wanted. Everything we have come to believe about the good life would suggest that this suburban boom was good for happiness. Why didn't it work? And why was faith in this model so quick to evaporate? The urban shake-up that began with the mortgage crisis in 2008 hit the newest, shiniest, most sprawling parts of the American city the hardest. Peñalosa argued that too many rich societies had used their wealth in ways that exacerbate urban problems rather than solve them.[134]

Could this help explain the happiness paradox? It's certainly a good time to consider the idea, now that tens of thousands of freshly paved cul-de-sacs across the United States have passed six springs without sprouting new homes. From the United States to Ireland to Spain, communities on the edge of suburban sprawl, that most American of forms, have yet to regain their pre-crash value. The future of cities is uncertain. It reached a rare moment in history where societies and markets appear to be teetering between the status quo and a radical change in how we live and design our lives in cities.[135]

According to Montgomery, if we are going to avoid the cataclysmic effects of global warming, we must find more efficient ways to build and live. Of course, it is not sure that a rush back to urban density will produce better lives than suburban dispersal. But the happy city theory presents an alluring possibility. If a flawed and broken city such as Bogotá can be reconfigured to produce more joy, then indeed it's possible to apply happy city principles to the wounds of wealthy places.[136] And if more extravagant, private, polluting, and energy-hungry communities have failed to deliver on happiness, then the search for a happier city might well be expected to reveal a greener, more resilient city, a place that saves the world while protecting our own lives. If there was a science behind it, presumably, that science could also be used to show how all of us might renovate good feelings in our communities.[137] Of course, Peñalosa's rhetoric is not science; it raises as many questions as it answers. Its inspirational qualities do not constitute proof of the city's power to make or break happiness, any more than the Beatles' "All You Need Is Love" is proof that all you do need is love. To test the idea, you would have to decide what you meant by happiness, and you would need a way to measure it.[138] So, you would have to understand how a road, a bus, a park, or a building might contribute to good feelings. You would have to tabulate the psychological effects of driving in traffic or catching the eye of a stranger on the sidewalk, or pausing in a pocket park, or of feeling crowded or lonely, or of the simple feeling that the city you live in is a good or bad place. You would have to go beyond politics and philosophy to find a map of the ingredients of happiness if it exists at all.[139]

The quest led me to some of the world's most significant and most miserable streets. It taught me through the labyrinths of neuroscience and behavioural economics. Urbanist found clues in paving stones, on rail lines, and on roller coasters, in architecture, in the stories of strangers who shared their lives with me, and in my urban experiments.[140]

According to Montgomery, one memory from early in the journey has stuck with him, perhaps because it carries both the sweetness and the

THE TIME OF CITY ECONOMICS

subjective slipperiness of the happiness we sometimes find in cities.

Nearly a million of them had stayed home that morning. Yes, it was el día sin carro, the car-free experiment that had grown into a yearly ritual. At first, the streets felt slightly eerie, like landscapes from a postapocalyptic Twilight Zone episode. All the rumble and roar of the city quieted. Gradually we expanded into the space left by the cars. It was as though an immense tension had been lifted from Bogotá, as though the city could finally shake out its exhaustion and breathe. The sky was a piercing blue.[141]

According to Montgomery, a bright-eyed ten-year-old pushed a miniature version of Peñalosa's bicycle through the crowd. The guy had been rushing to pick up his son from school, as other parents were doing that very moment all up and down the time zone. Millions of minivans, motorbikes, hatchbacks, and buses were congregating outside schools from Toronto to Tampa at this very moment—the same ritual, the same drumming of steering wheels, the same stop and go, the same corralling and ferrying of children.

16

Integral city

Integral City: evolutionary intelligence for the human hive; is a book by Marilyn Hamilton. It posits a concept called the "Integral City," a city as a living human system. It is architecture and city planning based on Integral Theory.

An *Integral City* paradigm views the city as a whole living system. It is the Human Hive. Like the beehive is for the honey bee species, the Integral City is the human species' collective habitat. An Integral City integrates qualities that create optimal conditions for social innovation and the emergence and ecoregional resilience.[142]

An *Integral City*:

- Builds capacity in the Individual (Inner and Outer)
- Builds capacity in the Collective (Culture and Structures)
- Develops Inquiry intelligence for generative exchanges
- Catalyzes Meshworking strategies to bridge sectors, silos, stovepipes & solitudes
- Designs feedback and feed-forward loops for Navigational direction
- Responds to critical Contexts: Ecospherical, Emerging, Integral,

Living
- Expresses Evolutionary Intelligence

An *Integral City* meshwork evolutionary intelligence to think about, actin, relate to and work towards creating the future's healthy city as creating the Human Hive. We view an Integral City through four perspectives, with systems thinking level of awareness.[143]

Integral City serves all those who are interested in creating vibrant, healthy and happy cities, primarily in four broad sectors:

- Urban professionals: Those involved in creating, maintaining and growing cities, within and outside government structures
- Businesses: Doing business in cities
- Non-profits and NGOs: Serving social and religious missions in cities
- Information and cultural organizations: Those involved in their cities' news, information, arts and entertainment

Within these categories, we offer information, training and services that meet the needs of a wide range of interest, authority and influence, from front-line practitioners, to decision-makers, to "deal makers" and high-level influencers.[144]

Integral City has an inspirational and comprehensive vision and mission. We live by a Master Code and a clear set of principles and values for how we engage in the world. We encourage you to learn more by visiting the Vision, Master Code, Mission and Values page.[145]

Author of *Integral City: Evolutionary Intelligence for the Human Hive*, and the Integral City book series, Dr Marilyn Hamilton is the Founder of Integral City Meshworks Inc., and TDG Holdings Inc. Marilyn leads a practice community using Integral City frameworks and practical tools to support multi-stakeholder groups in transforming their whole city and ecoregion into habitats that are as sustainable and resilient for humans as the beehive is for bees. Her Integral City approach incubates transformation strategies for City Staff, Civic Leaders, Civil Society, Business Entrepreneurs and Community Participants that integrate their contributions with Purpose, Place, Priorities, People and Planet.[146]

As Thought Leader and Project Leader Marilyn calls herself an "AQtivator." Marilyn leads teams to develop integrated resilience strategies that optimize official city plans and sustainability goals. She aligns multiple capacities with Environmental, Economic, Social and Cultural Capitals. She energizes Community Engagement, focuses on decision-making, and designs Dashboards for Monitoring City Performance and Managing Risk.

17

Future cities

The future of cities is a means to describe a series of enquiries, reviews and investigations into the likely requirements of cities in the future, the roles they will play, the pressures and threats they will address, and the trends that will help cities adjust and succeed. Future City is a term used to imagine what cities themselves will be like, how they will operate, what systems will orchestrate them and how they will relate to their stakeholders.

Each city is unique in detail but resembles others in function and pattern. Cities are the focal points in the occupation and utilization of the earth by man. Both a product of and an influence on surrounding regions develop in definite patterns in response to economic and social needs. Cities are also paradoxes. Their rapid growth and large size testify to their superiority as a technique for exploiting the earth. Yet, by their very success and consequent large extent, they often provide a low local environment for man.[147] The problem is to build the future city so that the advantages of urban concentration can be preserved for man's benefit and the disadvantages minimized.[148]

For as long as data have been generated about cities, various kinds of data-informed urbanism have occurred. In this paper, Kitchin argues that a new era is presently unfolding wherein data-informed urbanism is increasingly being complemented and replaced by data-driven, networked urbanism.[149] Cities are becoming ever more instrumented and networked. Their systems are interlinked and integrated, and vast troves of big urban data are being generated and used to manage and control urban life in real-time. Data-driven, networked urbanism, is the critical mode of production for what has widely been termed smart cities. In this paper, Kitchin provides a critical overview of data-driven, networked urbanism and smart cities focusing in particular on the relationship between data and the city (rather than network infrastructure or computational or urban issues), and critically examine several urban data issues including the politics of urban data; data owner-the ship, data control, data coverage and access; data security and data integrity; data protection and privacy, dataveillance, and data use such as social sorting and anticipatory governance; and technical data issues such as data quality, the veracity of data models and data analytics, and data integration and interoperability. Kitchin concludes that whilst data-driven, networked urbanism purports to produce a commonsensical, pragmatic, neutral, apolitical, evidence-based form of responsive urban governance, it is selective, craft flawed, normative and politically-inflected. Consequently, whilst data-driven, networked urbanism provides a set of solutions for urban problems, it does so within limitations and in the service of particular interests.[150]

New, "big" data sources allow measurement of city characteristics and outcome variables higher frequencies and finer geographic scales than ever before. However, big data will not solve broad urban social science questions on its own. Big data has the most value for studying cities when it allows measurement of the previously opaque, or when it can be coupled with exogenous shocks to people or place.[151] Glaeser describes several new urban data sources and illustrates how they can improve cities' study and function. Glaeser, Kominers, S Luca, and Naik, show

how Google Street View images can be used to predict income in New York City, suggesting that similar image data can be used to map wealth and poverty previously unmeasured areas of the developing world. Glaeser discusses how survey techniques can be improved to better measure willingness to pay for urban amenities. They explain how Internet data is being used to improve the quality of city services.[152]

From 1940 to 1990, Shapiro's research showed a 10 per cent increase in a metropolitan area's concentration of college-educated residents was associated with a .6 per cent increase in subsequent employment growth. Using data on growth in wages and house values, Shapiro's paper attempts to distinguish between explanations for this correlation based on local productivity growth and explanations based on growth in local consumption amenities.[153] Calibration of a city growth model suggests that roughly two-thirds of human capital's growth effect is due to enhanced productivity growth. A change in life quality causes the rest. This contrasts with the standard argument that social capital generates growth in urban areas solely through local knowledge spillovers.

"Smart cities" is a term that has gained traction in academia, business and government to describe cities that, on the one hand, are increasingly composed of and monitored by pervasive and ubiquitous computing and, on the other, whose economy and governance are being driven by innovation, creativity and entrepreneurship, enacted by smart people.[154] Kitchin's paper focuses on the former and how cities are being instrumented with digital devices and infrastructure that produce 'big data' which enable real-time analysis of city life, new modes of technocratic urban governance, and a re-imagining of cities. Kitchin's analysis details several projects that seek to produce real-time analysis of the town and provides a critical reflection on the implications of big data and smart urbanism.

18

Still same city

My conclusion is that managing needs to adapt ta a changing world and its inner focus be superseded by the notion of urban strategy. This is easier said than done will require much ingenuity.

In his book Diversity and Complexity, Scott E. Page explains, "Complexity can be loosely thought of as interesting structures and patterns that are not easily described or predicted.[155] Systems that produce complexity consist of diverse rule-following entities whose behaviours are interdependent. Those entities interact over a contact structure or network. Also, the entities often adapt." Understanding complexity is essential because sometimes things are not further reducible. While Occam's Razor's premise is that something should be made as simple as possible but not simpler, sometimes some things cannot be reduced. There is, in fact, a minimum. Certain items can be appropriately contemplated only in all their complicated, interconnected glory.

Cities are complex adaptive systems. They cannot be created for success from the top-down by the imposition of simple rules. In her seminal book The Death and Life of Great American Cities, Jane Jacobs approached the city as a complex adaptive system, turned city planning on its head, and likely saved many North American cities by taking them apart and showing that they cannot be reduced to a series of simple behavioural interactions.[156]

Cities fall precisely into the definition of Complexity given above by Page. They are full of rule-following humans, cars, and wildlife, the behaviours of which are interdependent on the other entities and respond to feedback. These city components interact over multiple interfaces in a city net-work and adapt quickly, changing their behaviour based on food availability, road closures, or perceived safety. But the city itself cannot be understood by looking at just one of these behaviours. Jacobs starts with *"the kind of problem which cities pose — a problem in handling organized complexity"* — and a series of observations about that standard, almost innocuous, part of all cities: the sidewalk. Cities have become central to our species, with an increasing majority of people living in them and producing most of our globalized society's wealth.

In conclusion, the management of cities must evolve to meet the challenges of a rapidly changing world, shifting its focus from mere administration to strategic urban planning. This transition requires not only vision but also a great deal of ingenuity.

Cities, with their myriad interactions and feedback loops, epitomize complexity. From the bustling sidewalks to the bustling streets, every aspect of urban life is intertwined, responding to changes in real-time. Yet, it is this very complexity that fuels innovation, creativity, and progress.

As we look to the future, it is imperative that urban management acknowledges and embraces the inherent complexity of cities. By doing so, we can foster environments that are adaptable, resilient, and conducive to the flourishing of all inhabitants. The journey ahead may be challenging, but by embracing complexity, we pave the way for vibrant, thriving cities that truly serve the needs of their diverse populations.

Notes

INTRODUCTION

1. Friedmann, J. (2002), *The prospect of cities*, U of Minnesota Press, Pumain, D. (2006), Alternative explanations of hierarchical differentiation in urban systems, In *Hierarchy in natural and social sciences* (pp. 169-222), Springer, Dordrecht.

2. Freire, M., & Polese, M. (2003), *Connecting Cities with Macro-economic Concerns: The Missing Link*, The World Bank, Polèse, M. (2005), Cities and national economic growth: a reappraisal, *Urban Studies*, 42(8), 1429-1451.

3. Heer, F. (1962), *The medieval world*.

4. Polèse, M. (2005), Cities and national economic growth: a reappraisal, *urban Studies*, 42(8), 1429-1451.

CITY ECONOMICS

5. Plummer, P., & Sheppard, E. (2006), Geography matters: agency, structures and dynamics at the intersection of economics and geography, *Journal of Economic Geography*, 6(5), 619-637.

6. Gorter, C., & Nijkamp, P. (2001), Location theory, *International encyclopedia for the social and behavioural sciences*, 9013-9019.

7. Zukin, S. (1995), *The cultures of cities* (Vol. 150), Oxford: Blackwell.

8. Henderson, V., & Thisse, J. F. (Eds.). (2004), *Handbook of regional and urban economics: cities and geography* (Vol. 4), Elsevier.

9. Johansson, B., & Forslund, U. (2008), The analysis of location, co-location and urbanisation economies, *Handbook of Research on Cluster Theory*, 1, 39-66.

10. Florida, R. (2014), The creative class and economic development, *Economic development quarterly*, 28(3), 196-205.

ORDINARY CITIES

11. Amin, A., & Graham, S. (1997), The ordinary city, *Transactions of the Institute of British Geographers*, 22(4), 411-429.

12. Amin, A., & Graham, S. (1997), The ordinary city, *Transactions of the Institute of British Geographers*, 22(4), 411-429.

13 Gemmiti, R. (2019), Ordinary Cities, *The Wiley Blackwell Encyclopedia of Urban and Regional Studies*, 1-6, Amin, A., & Graham, S. (1997), The ordinary city, *Transactions of the Institute of British Geographers*, 22(4), 411-429.

14 Robinson, J. (2015), World cities, or a world of ordinary cities?. *Cities of the Global South reader*, 66-72, Robinson, J. (2006), *Ordinary cities: between modernity and development*, Psychology Press.

15 Robinson, J. (2002), Global and world cities: a view from off the map, *International journal of urban and regional research*, 26(3), 531-554.

16 Robinson, J. (2006), *Ordinary cities: between modernity and development*, Psychology Press.

17 Robinson, J. (2006), *Ordinary cities: Between modernity and development*. Psychology Press, Robinson, J. (2002), Global and world cities: a view from off the map. *International journal of urban and regional research*, 26(3), 531-554.

18 Schuermans, N. (2009), J. Robinson, Ordinary cities: Between Modernity and Development, London, Routledge, 2006, xiv+ 204 p. *Belgeo. Revue belge de géographie*, (1).

CULTURAL CITY

19 Agnew, J., Mercer, J., & Sopher, D. (Eds.). (2013), *The city in cultural context*, Routledge, Rosenstein, C. (2011), Cultural development and city neighbourhoods, *City, culture and society*, 2(1), 9-15.

20 Leach, E. (1976), *Culture and Communication: the logic by which symbols are connected, An introduction to the use of structuralist analysis in social anthropology*, Cambridge University Press.

21 Evans, G. (2003), Hard-branding the cultural city—from Prado to Prada, *International journal of urban and regional research*, 27(2), 417-440, Yeoh, B. S. (2005), The global cultural city? Spatial imagineering and politics in the (multi) cultural marketplaces of South-east Asia, *Urban Studies*, 42(5-6), 945-958.

22 Agnew, J., Mercer, J., & Sopher, D. (Eds.). (2013), *The city in cultural context*, Routledge.

23 Ryan, M. T., Hutchison, R., & Gottdiener, M. (2018), *The new urban sociology*, Routledge.

24 Ryan, M. T., Hutchison, R., & Gottdiener, M. (2018), *The new urban sociology*, Routledge, Archer, K. (2013), *The city: the basics*, Routledge, Baumeister, R., & Lee, S. (Eds.). (2007), *The domestic and the foreign in architecture*, 010 Publishers, Sorkin, M. (1991), *Exquisite corpse: Writing on buildings*, Verso.

25 Featherstone, M. (1994), City cultures and post-modern lifestyles, *Post-Fordism: A Reader*, 387-408, Scott, A. J. (1999), The cultural economy: geography and the creative field, *Media, culture & society*, 21(6), 807-817.

NOTES

26 Gleeson, B. (2014), *The urban condition*, Routledge.
27 Featherstone, M. (1994), City cultures and post-modern lifestyles, *Post-Fordism: A Reader*, 387-408, Scott, A. J. (2000), *The cultural economy of cities: essays on the geography of image-producing industries*, Sage.
28 Agnew, J., Mercer, J., & Sopher, D. (Eds.). (2013), *The city in cultural context*. Routledge.
29 Gottdiener, M. (2010), *The social production of urban space*, University of Texas Press.
30 Ryan, M. T., Hutchison, R., & Gottdiener, M. (2018), *The new urban sociology*, Routledge, Archer, K. (2013), *The city: the basics*, Routledge.
31 Castells, M. (2011), *The rise of the network society* (Vol. 12), John wiley & sons, Bruhn, J. G. (2011), *The sociology of community connections*, Springer Science & Business Media.
32 Banks, M., Lovatt, A., O'connor, J., & Raffo, C. (2000), Risk and trust in the cultural industries, *Geoforum*, 31(4), 453-464, Van Aalst, I. (1997), *Cultuur in de stad: Over de rol van culturele voorzieningen in de ontwikkeling van stadscentra* (Doctoral dissertation, Jan van Arkel).
33 Bruhn, J. G. (2011), *The sociology of community connections*, Springer Science & Business Media, Rossi, U. (2017), *Cities in global capitalism*, John Wiley & Sons.
34 Forester, J. (1980), Critical theory and planning practice, *Journal of the American Planning Association*, 46(3), 275-286, Gottdiener, M. (2010), *The social production of urban space*, University of Texas Press.

WALKABLE CITY

35 Bornstein, D., & Davis, S. (2010), *Social entrepreneurship: What everyone needs to know*, Oxford University Press, Ries, E. (2011), *The lean startup: How today's entrepreneurs use continuous innovation to create radically successful businesses*, Currency.
36 Leinberger, C. B. (2010), *The option of urbanism: Investing in a new American dream*, Island Press.
37 Speck, J. (2013), *Walkable city: How downtown can save America, one step at a time*, macmillan.
38 Speck, J. (2013), *Walkable city: How downtown can save America, one step at a time*, macmillan.
39 McNichol, T. (2004), Roads gone wild, *Wired Magazine*, 12(12), 108-112.
40 Mapes, J. (2009), Pedaling revolution, *Portland, OR: Portland State University*.
41 Owen, D. (2014), *Green metropolis*, EGEA spa.
42 McNichol, T. (2004), Roads Gone Wild No street signs. No sidewalks. No accidents. How making driving seem more dangerous could make it safer. *WIRED-SAN FRANCISCO-*, 12(12), 108-112.

INDUSTRIAL CITY

43 Scott, A. J. (2000), *The cultural economy of cities: essays on the geography of image-producing industries*, Sage, Short, J. R., Benton, L. M., Luce, W. B., & Walton, J. (1993), Reconstructing the image of an industrial city, *Annals of the Association of American Geographers*, 83(2), 207-224.

44 Manzoni, C. (2014), *Cultural and Creative Industries as key factors for Chinese economic development, Analysis of Beijing and Shanghai* (Bachelor's thesis, Università Ca'Foscari Venezia).

45 Evans, G. (2009), Creative cities, creative spaces and urban policy, *Urban studies*, 46(5-6), 1003-1040.

46 Evans, G. (2009), Creative cities, creative spaces and urban policy, *Urban studies*, 46(5-6), 1003-1040, Amore, A. (2019), *Tourism and urban regeneration: Processes compressed in time and space*, Routledge.

CREATIVE CITY

47 David George Druce Yencken (June 3, 1931 – September 21, 2019), was a builder, businessman, academic and heritage practitioner in Australia.

48 Yencken, D. (1988), "The creative city," *Meanjin*, 47.

49 Anttiroiko, A. V. (2014), *The political economy of city branding*, Routledge, Landry, C. (2005), Lineages of the creative city, *Creativity and the City, Ne,*

50 Landry, C. (2012), *The creative city: A toolkit for urban innovators*, Earthscan.

51 Brouillette, S. (2014), *Literature and the creative economy*, Stanford University Press, Da Costa, D. (2016), *Politicizing creative economy: activism and a hunger called theater*, University of Illinois Press.

52 McRobbie, A. (2018), *Be creative: Making a living in the new culture industries*, John Wiley & Sons.

53 McRobbie, A. (2018), *Be creative: Making a living in the new culture industries*, John Wiley & Sons, Richards, G., & Duif, L. (2018), *Small cities with big dreams: Creative placemaking and branding strategies*, Routledge, Johnson, D. (2013), *Media franchising: Creative license and collaboration in the culture industries* (Vol. 11), NYU Press.

54 Kong, L. (2020), From cultural industries to creative industries and back? Towards clarifying theory and rethinking policy, In *Handbook on the Geographies of Creativity*, Edward Elgar Publishing, Yue, A. (2006), Cultural governance and creative industries in Singapore, *International journal of cultural policy*, 12(1), 17-33.

55 Landry, C. (2012), *The creative city: A toolkit for urban innovators*, Earthscan, O'brien, D. (2013), *Cultural policy: Management, value and modernity in the creative industries*, Routledge.

NOTES

56 Howkins, J. (2002), *The creative economy: How people make money from ideas*, Penguin UK.

57 Florida, R. (2014), *The rise of the creative class—revisited: Revised and expanded*, Basic Books (AZ).

58 Peck, J. (2005), Struggling with the creative class, *International journal of urban and regional research*, 29(4), 740-770.

59 Florida, R. (2014), *The rise of the creative class—revisited: Revised and expanded*, Basic Books (AZ), Florida, R. (1995), Toward the learning region, *Futures*, 27(5), 527-536.

CONSUMER CITY

60 Costa, M. (2003), Potential hazards of hexavalent chromate in our drinking water, *Toxicology and applied pharmacology*, 188(1), 1-5.

61 Wynne, D., O'Connor, J., & Phillips, D. (1998), Consumption and the postmodern city, *Urban Studies*, 35(5-6), 841-864.

62 Glaeser, E. L., Kolko, J., & Saiz, A. (2001), Consumer city, *Journal of economic geography*, 1(1), 27-50, Glaeser, E. L. (1999), Learning in cities, *Journal of urban Economics*, 46(2), 254-277.

63 Glaeser, E.L., Kolko, J. and Saiz, A., (2001), Consumer city, *Journal of economic geography*, 1(1), pp.27-50. Vancouver

64 Kahn, S. (1997), Evidence of nominal wage stickiness from microdata, *The American Economic Review*, 87(5), 993-1008.

GREEN CITY

65 See U.S. Census Bureau, "Metropolitan and Micropolitan Statistical Areas," (www.census.gov/population/www/estimates/metroarea.html [October 2005]).

66 Kahn, M. E. (2007), *Green cities: urban growth and the environment*, Brookings Institution Press.

67 Kahn, M. E. (2007), *Green cities: urban growth and the environment*, Brookings Institution Press.

68 Simon Kuznets won the Nobel Prize in Economics in 1971. He studied the cross-national relationship between national per capita income and national income inequality and found evidence of a nonlinear pattern. Gene Grossman and Alan Krueger later identified a similar relationship between per capita income and pollution.

69 Kahn, M. E. (2007), *Green cities: urban growth and the environment*, Brookings Institution Press, Chapter 3.

HEALTHY CITY

70 Chadwick, E., & Flinn, M. W. (1966), *Report on the sanitary condition of the laboring population of Great Britain*, 1842.

71 Duffy, T. P. (1993), The sooner the better, *New England Journal of Medicine*, 329(10), 710-713.

72 Pauly, M. V., McGuire, T. G., & Barros, P. P. (Eds.) (2012), *Handbook of health economics* (Vol. 2), Elsevier.

73 Goddard, J., & Puukka, J. (2008), The engagement of higher education institutions in regional development: An overview of the opportunities and challenges, *Higher education management and policy*, 20(2), 11-41, Evans, G. (2002), *Cultural planning: An urban renaissance?*, Routledge.

74 McGranahan, G., Balk, D., & Anderson, B. (2007), The rising tide: assessing the risks of climate change and human settlements in low elevation coastal zones, *Environment and urbanization*, 19(1), 17-37.

75 Pelling, M. (2003), *Natural disaster and development in a globalizing world*, Routledge, p.7.

76 Carta, M. G., Coppo, P., Reda, M. A., Hardoy, M. C., & Carpiniello, B. (2001), Depression and social change, From transcultural psychiatry to a constructivist model, *Epidemiology and Psychiatric Sciences*, 10(1), 46-58.

MEGACITY

77 Spivak, G. C. (2000), Megacity, *Grey Room*, 8-25, Henderson, J. V. (2010), Cities and development. *Journal of regional science*, 50(1), 515-540, Fox, S. (2012), Urbanization as a global historical process: Theory and evidence from sub-Saharan Africa, *Population and Development Review*, 38(2), 285-310.

78 Fuchs, R. J., Brennan, E., Lo, F. C., Uitto, J. I., & Chamie, J. (Eds.). (1994), *Mega-city Growth and the Future*, United Nations University Press, Rogers, R. (2008), *Cities for a small planet*, Basic Books, Clark, D. (2003), *Urban world/global city*, Psychology Press, Jedwab, R., & Vollrath, D. (2015), Urbanization without growth in historical perspective, *Explorations in Economic History*, 58, 1-21.

79 Bertaud, A., & Malpezzi, S. (2003), The spatial distribution of population in 48 world cities: Implications for economies in transition, *Center for urban land economics research, University of Wisconsin*, 32(1), 54-55.

80 Potere, D., & Schneider, A. (2007), A critical look at representations of urban areas in global maps. *GeoJournal*, 69(1-2), 55-80, Clark, D. (2003), *Urban world/global city*, Psychology Press.

81 Griffiths, P., Hostert, P., Gruebner, O., & van der Linden, S. (2010), Mapping megacity growth with multi-sensor data, *Remote Sensing of Environment*, 114(2), 426-439, Un-

Habitat. (2012), *State of the World's Cities 2008/9: Harmonious Cities*, Routledge, Setchell, C. A. (1995), The growing environmental crisis in the world's mega cities: the case of Bangkok, *Third World Planning Review*, 17(1), 1.

82 Bronger, D. (1996), Megastädte. *Geographische Rundschau*, 48, 74-81.

83 Ditzen, B., Schaer, M., Gabriel, B., Bodenmann, G., Ehlert, U., & Heinrichs, M. (2009), Intranasal oxytocin increases positive communication and reduces cortisol levels during couple conflict. *Biological psychiatry*, 65(9), 728-731.

84 Ryu, Y. H., Baik, J. J., & Lee, S. H. (2013), Effects of anthropogenic heat on ozone air quality in a megacity, *Atmospheric environment*, 80, 20-30.

85 Sassen, S. (2002), Global cities and survival circuits, *American studies: An anthology*, 185-193.

86 Hazel, M. M. GlobeScan, (2007), *Desafíos de las Megaciudades, Bogotá: Gatos Gemelos Ltda.*

87 Heinrichs, D., Krellenberg, K., & Hansjürgens, B. (2012), Introduction: Megacities in Latin America as risk habitat, In *Risk Habitat Megacity* (pp. 3-17), Springer, Berlin, Heidelberg,Webster, D. (2004), New drivers, new outcomes, *Thailand beyond the Crisis*, 7, 285.

88 Brugmans, G. (2010), *Megacities: Exploring a sustainable future*, 010 Publishers.

89 Castells, M. (2011), *The rise of the network society* (Vol. 12), John wiley & sons, Curtis, S. (2016), *Global cities and global order*, Oxford University Press.

90 Porter, M. E. (2000), Location, competition, and economic development: Local clusters in a global economy, *Economic development quarterly*, 14(1), 15-34.

CHARTER CITY

91 Romer, P. (2010), *Technologies, rules, and progress: The case for charter cities*, (No. id: 2471).

92 Romer, P. (2015), Romer on urbanization, charter cities, and growth theory. Interview with Paul Romer conducted by Brandon Fuller. *Blog. New York: Marron Institute of Urban Management, New York University.* Accessed February, 14, 2019.

93 Cheong, K. C., & Goh, K. L. (2013), Hong Kong as charter city prototype–When concept meets reality, *Cities*, 35, 100-103, Romer, P. (2015), Romer on urbanization, charter cities, and growth theory. Interview with Paul Romer conducted by Brandon Fuller, *Blog, New York: Marron Institute of Urban Management, New York University. Accessed February, 14, 2019.*

94 Romer, P. (2010), *Technologies, rules, and progress: The case for charter cities*, (No. id: 2471).

STARTUP CITY

95 Feld, B. (2020), *Startup communities: Building an entrepreneurial ecosystem in your city*, John Wiley & Sons.

96 Cohan, P. S., Cohan, P. S., & Ramachandran (2018), *Startup Cities*, Apress.

97 Lee, C. M. (2000), *The Silicon Valley edge: A habitat for innovation and entrepreneurship*, Stanford University Press.

98 Cohan, P. S., Cohan, P. S., & Ramachandran. (2018), *Startup Cities*, Apress, Wisnioski, M., Hintz, E. S., & Kleine, M. S. (Eds.), (2019), *Does America Need More Innovators?* MIT Press.

99 Cappelli, P. (2008), Talent management for the twenty-first century, *Harvard business review*, 86(3), 74.

100 Cohan, P. S. (2018), What Is the Startup Common?, In *Startup Cities* (pp. 3-14), Apress, Berkeley, CA, Cohan, P. S., Cohan, P. S., & Ramachandran, (2018), *Startup Cities*, Apress.

101 Cohan, P. S. (2018), What Is the Startup Common?, In *Startup Cities* (pp. 3-14), Apress, Berkeley, CA, Cohan, P. S., Cohan, P. S., & Ramachandran, (2018), *Startup Cities*, Apress.

102 Cohan, P. S. (2018), What Is the Startup Common?, In *Startup Cities* (pp. 3-14), Apress, Berkeley, CA, Cohan, P. S., Cohan, P. S., & Ramachandran, (2018), *Startup Cities*, Apress.

103 Feld, B. (2020), *Startup communities: Building an entrepreneurial ecosystem in your city*, John Wiley & Sons, Florida, R., Adler, P., King, K., & Mellander, C. (2020). The city as startup machine: the urban underpinnings of modern entrepreneurship, In *Urban Studies and Entrepreneurship* (pp. 19-30), Springer, Cham.

SMART CITY

104 Cocchia, A. (2014), Smart and digital city: A systematic literature review, In *Smart city* (pp. 13-43), Springer, Cham.

105 Dameri, R. P. (2013), Searching for smart city definition: a comprehensive proposal, *International Journal of computers & technology*, 11(5), 2544-2551.

106 Dameri, R. P., & Rosenthal-Sabroux, C. (2014),. Smart city and value creation, In *Smart city* (pp. 1-12), Springer, Cham, Dameri, R. P. (2013), Searching for smart city definition: a comprehensive proposal, *International Journal of computers & technology*, 11(5), 2544-2551.

107 Devlin, J. M. (2016), *Revitalizing Downtown Houston-Bringing Back the Human Scale* (Doctoral dissertation, Virginia Tech), Speck, J. (2013), *Walkable city: How downtown can save America, one step at a time*, macmillan.

108 Dameri, R. P., & Rosenthal-Sabroux, C. (2014), Smart city and value creation, In *Smart city* (pp. 1-12), Springer, Cham.

NOTES

109 Ruiz Andrade, M. (2020), *Chandigarh's modern citizens, India's smart citizenry:(re) constituting subalternity* (Master's thesis, Humboldt-Universität zu Berlin).

110 Benevolo, C., Dameri, R. P., & D'auria, B. (2016), Smart mobility in smart city, In *Empowering Organizations* (pp. 13-28), Springer, Cham.

111 Dameri, R. P. (2017), Smart city implementation, *Progress in IS; Springer: Genoa, Italy.*

112 Sadowski, J., & Pasquale, F. A. (2015), The spectrum of control: A social theory of the smart city, *First Monday, 20*(7), de Oliveira, T. H. M., & Painho, M. (2020), Open Geospatial Data Contribution Towards Sentiment Analysis Within the Human Dimension of Smart Cities, In *Open Source Geospatial Science for Urban Studies* (pp. 75-95), Springer, Cham.

113 Cocchia, A. (2014), Smart and digital city: A systematic literature review, In *Smart city* (pp. 13-43), Springer, Cham.

114 Bhushan, B., Khamparia, A., Sagayam, K. M., Sharma, S. K., Ahad, M. A., & Debnath, N. C. (2020), Blockchain for smart cities: A review of architectures, integration trends and future research directions, *Sustainable Cities and Society, 61*, 102360.

115 Batty, M., Axhausen, K. W., Giannotti, F., Pozdnoukhov, A., Bazzani, A., Wachowicz, M., ... & Portugali, Y. (2012), Smart cities of the future, *The European Physical Journal Special Topics, 214*(1), 481-518.

116 Vermesan, O., & Friess, P. (Eds.). (2013), *Internet of things: converging technologies for smart environments and integrated ecosystems*, River publishers. Anthopoulos, L. G. (2017), *Understanding smart cities: A tool for smart government or an industrial trick?* (Vol. 22), Cham: Springer International Publishing.

117 Söderström, O., Paasche, T., & Klauser, F. (2014), Smart cities as corporate storytelling, *City, 18*(3), 307-320.

118 Anthopoulos, L. G. (2017), *Understanding smart cities: A tool for smart government or an industrial trick?* (Vol. 22), Cham: Springer International Publishing, Sepe, M. (2013), *Planning and place in the city: Mapping place identity*, Routledge.

119 Anthopoulos, L. G. (2017), *Understanding smart cities: A tool for smart government or an industrial trick?* (Vol. 22), Cham: Springer International Publishing, Söderström, O., Paasche, T., & Klauser, F. (2014), Smart cities as corporate storytelling, *City, 18*(3), 307-320, Dameri, R. P., & Rosenthal-Sabroux, C. (2014), Smart city and value creation, In *Smart city* (pp. 1-12), Springer, Cham.

120 Benevolo, C., Dameri, R. P., & D'auria, B. (2016), Smart mobility in smart city, In *Empowering Organizations* (pp. 13-28), Springer, Cham.

121 Cocchia, A. (2014), Smart and digital city: A systematic literature review, In *Smart city* (pp. 13-43), Springer, Cham, Benevolo, C., Dameri, R. P., & D'auria, B. (2016), Smart mobility in smart city, In *Empowering Organizations* (pp. 13-28), Springer, Cham.

122 Dameri, R. P. (2017), Smart city definition, goals and performance, In *Smart City Implementation* (pp. 1-22), Springer, Cham.

123 Söderström, O., Paasche, T., & Klauser, F. (2014), Smart cities as corporate storytelling, *City*, 18(3), 307-320.

124 Benevolo, C., Dameri, R. P., & D'auria, B. (2016), Smart mobility in smart city, In *Empowering Organizations* (pp. 13-28), Springer, Cham.

125 Dameri, R. P. (2017), Smart city definition, goals and performance, In *Smart City Implementation* (pp. 1-22), Springer, Cham.

126 Neirotti, P., De Marco, A., Cagliano, A. C., Mangano, G., & Scorrano, F. (2014), Current trends in Smart City initiatives: Some stylised facts, *Cities*, 38, 25-36.

127 Picon, A. (2015), *Smart cities: a spatialised intelligence*, John Wiley & Sons.

128 Dameri, R. P. (2017), Smart city implementation, *Progress in IS*; Springer: Genoa, Italy.

HAPPY CITY

129 Montgomery, C. (2013), *Happy city: Transforming our lives through urban design*, Macmillan.

130 Ballas, D. (2013), What makes a 'happy city'?, *Cities*, 32, S39-S50.

131 Dawson, A. (2017), *Extreme cities: The peril and promise of urban life in the age of climate change*, Verso Books, Register, R. (2006), *Ecocities: Rebuilding cities in balance with nature*, New Society Publishers.

132 Montgomery, C. (2013), *Happy city: Transforming our lives through urban design*, Macmillan.

133 Resnik, D. B. (2007), *The price of truth: How money affects the norms of science*, Oxford University Press.

134 Stimson, J. (2018), *Public opinion in America: Moods, cycles, and swings*, Routledge.

135 Chaddha, A., & Wilson, W. J. (2011), "Way down in the hole": systemic urban inequality and The Wire. *Critical Inquiry*, 38(1), 164-188, Montgomery, C. (2013), *Happy city: Transforming our lives through urban design*, Macmillan.

136 Register, R. (2006), *Ecocities: Rebuilding cities in balance with nature*, New Society Publishers, Barber, B. R. (2013), *If mayors ruled the world: Dysfunctional nations, rising cities*, Yale University Press.

137 Montgomery, C. (2013), *Happy city: Transforming our lives through urban design*, Macmillan.

138 Montgomery, C. (2013), *Happy city: Transforming our lives through urban design*, Macmillan.

NOTES

139 Ellard, C. (2015), *Places of the heart: The psychogeography of everyday life*, Bellevue literary press, Pickett, K., & Wilkinson, R. (2010), *The spirit level: Why equality is better for everyone*, Penguin UK.

140 Harford, T. (2017), *Messy: The power of disorder to transform our lives*, Penguin, Mak, G. (2008), *In Europe: travels through the twentieth century*, Vintage.

141 Montgomery, C. (2013), *Happy city: Transforming our lives through urban design*, Macmillan.

INTEGRAL CITY

142 Hamilton, M. (2009), *Integral city: Evolutionary intelligences for the human hive*, New Society Publishers, Schieffer, A., & Lessem, R. (2016), *Integral development: Realising the transformative potential of individuals, Organisations and societies*, Routledge.

143 Hamilton, M. (2009), *Integral city: Evolutionary intelligences for the human hive*, New Society Publishers, Hamilton, M., & Sanders, B. (2014), THE INTEGRAL CITY 2.0 ONLINE CONFERENCE, *Journal of Integral Theory & Practice*, 9(1).

144 Ferguson, B. K. (2012), A unified model for integral city design, *Management of Environmental Quality: An International Journal*.

145 Lessem, R., & Schieffer, A. (2016), *Integral economics: Releasing the economic genius of your society*, CRC Press, Hamilton, M. (2009), *Integral city: Evolutionary intelligences for the human hive*, New Society Publishers.

146 Hamilton, M. (2009), *Integral city: Evolutionary intelligences for the human hive*, New Society Publishers.

FUTURE CITIES

147 University of Chicago. College, & Harris, C. D. (1961), *The nature of cities*. Syllabus Division, University of Chicago Press, Potter, R. B., & Lloyd-Evans, S. (2014), *The city in the developing world*, Routledge.

148 Harris, C. D. (1961), *The nature of cities*, Syllabus Division, University of Chicago Press.

149 Kitchin, R. (2014), The real-time city? big data and smart urbanism, *GeoJournal*, 79(1):1–14.

150 Kitchin, R. (2015), *Data-driven, networked urbanism*.

151 Glaeser, E. L., Kominers, S. D., Luca, M., and Naik, N. (2018), Big data and big cities: The promises and limitations of improved measures of urban life, *Economic Inquiry*, 56(1):114–137.

152 Glaeser, E. L., Kominers, S. D., Luca, M., & Naik, N. (2018), Big data and big cities: The promises and limitations of improved measures of urban life, *Economic Inquiry*, 56(1), 114-137.

153 Shapiro, J. M. (2003), Smart cities: explaining the relationship between city growth and human capital, *Available at SSRN 480172*.

154 Kitchin, R. (2014), The real-time city? big data and smart urbanism, *GeoJournal*, 79(1):1–14, Kitchin, R. (2015), Data-driven, networked urbanism.

STILL SAME CITY

155 Page, S. E. (2010), *Diversity and complexity*, volume 2, Princeton University Press.

156 Jacobs, J. (2016), *The death and life of great American cities*, Vintage.

About the Author

You can connect with me on:
🐦 https://twitter.com/sergejavetisyan

www.ingramcontent.com/pod-product-compliance
Lightning Source LLC
Chambersburg PA
CBHW070259220526
45465CB00004B/1669